RECOVERING
FAITH

STORIES OF CATHOLICS
WHO CAME HOME

RECOVERING
FAITH

STORIES OF CATHOLICS
WHO CAME HOME

Lorene Hanley Duquin

Our Sunday Visitor Publishing Division
Our Sunday Visitor, Inc.
Huntington, IN 46750

For Colin, Ellie, and Patrick,
with lots of love

Table of Contents

INTRODUCTION

THIS BOOK IS A COLLECTION OF STORIES about people who have come back to the Catholic Church. The reasons why they left the Church are as varied as the people themselves:

- Some of them never really left. They kept going to Mass every week but felt disconnected, as if they were just going through the motions.
- Others drifted away as teens or young adults. Most of them weren't angry or upset with the Church. They just got out of the habit of going to Mass. They moved away from their childhood home. Their lives got busy. Their faith simply wasn't a priority.
- One left the Catholic Church because of an intellectual search for truth that led down a path of atheism.
- Interfaith marriage and divorce influenced the decisions of several people.
- Some embarked on a search for another church because they struggled with Catholic beliefs and teachings. Others turned to a Protestant church because they wanted to learn more about the Bible or find a welcoming faith community.
- One woman's search for God led her into New Age spirituality.
- Difficulty in reconciling the changes in the Church after the Second Vatican Council (1962-1965) was an issue for one person in this book.

- For a few, the decision to leave the Catholic Church was an emotional reaction to painful experiences or crises in their lives. Some were angry at God. Some were angry at the Church.

The circumstances surrounding their stories are all unique. But if you read closely, you will notice that every person in this book felt moved in one way or another to come back to the Catholic faith through the inspiration of the Holy Spirit. It was as if the Holy Spirit was nudging them with ideas, inspirations, and longings.

Sometimes, the Holy Spirit spoke to them in quiet revelations. Others were jolted by strange coincidences. A few experienced "aha!" moments in which they began to see and understand everything from a different perspective. Some began to question the meaning and purpose of their lives. Others began to feel as if they were being called to use their God-given gifts and talents in a more meaningful way.

Curiosity about Marian apparitions led a few people back to the Church. Others felt drawn after memories of their childhood faith experiences began to surface. Many began to feel a deep hunger for the Eucharist.

Family members and friends were instrumental in encouraging several people to come back to the Church. A few came back because of crises or important milestones in their lives.

You will see all of this and much more in their stories. You will also see that, in the end, each person in this book had to surrender in one way or another to the movement of the Holy Spirit in his or her life. They had to turn away from their old way of doing things and venture down a new path.

For some, the path back to the Catholic Church felt easy and natural. For others, it was more challenging. Some describe coming back to the Catholic Church as an event. Others describe it as a process.

A few of them lost friends because of their decision. One lost a prestigious position. Several had to reorient themselves to a Church that was very different from the Church they had left. A few had to forgive the Church for painful things that had happened in their past. Some had to forgive themselves for the things they had done.

But in every single instance, the decision to come back to the Catholic Church changed the lives of the people in this book. Two of them became priests, and one became a permanent deacon. A few had former marriages annulled. Almost all of them started new ministries or became actively involved in an existing ministry. Several discovered that their decision prompted others to become Catholic or return to the Church. All of them found what they describe as a new sense of purpose in life and a deep sense of peace.

They are sharing their stories because they know that there are many struggling Catholics who are feeling drawn back to the Church. They want you to know that it is possible to recover your faith. They hope that their stories will help you to see how the Holy Spirit is working in your life. They encourage you to move with the flow of God's grace and discover where the Holy Spirit is leading you.

You will find sidebars in each chapter. Many of these give encouragement or offer understanding and advice to Catholics who may be considering coming home. Informational sidebars give brief explanations of Catholic teachings or practices. Others identify persons, ministries, or movements.

Maybe you're reading this book because you've already felt the pull to come back to the Catholic Church. Maybe you're reading it because you have a family member or friend who is away from the Church. Maybe you just picked it up out of curiosity. Whatever the reason, may the Holy Spirit give you new insights and deeper understandings. May you be filled with God's grace. May you experience Christ's peace. May you grow in faith, hope, and love.

Teresa Tomeo

Teresa Tomeo is an author, columnist, syndicated Catholic radio talk-show host, and motivational speaker. Her daily morning program, Catholic Connection, is produced by Ave Maria Radio and is syndicated to more than 140 Catholic stations. She lives in Detroit with her husband, Dominic.

TERESA TOMEO was born into a traditional Italian-American family. Her parents were devout Catholics, but they were very much like most parents of the generation who believed that the religious education of children was the responsibility of priests and nuns. Teresa was baptized in St. Joan of Arc Church in St. Clair Shores, Michigan, and spent eight formative years in Catholic school.

By the time she entered the public high school, Teresa's formal religious education had ended. She attended Mass with her family but now admits that she was Catholic in the same way that she was Italian. "It was more cultural," she explains, "more ritualistic than a personal relationship with God."

As a freshman at Central Michigan University, Teresa had already started to drift away from the practice of her faith. She would go to Mass when she came home for holidays or when she was worried about an exam. "I didn't think I needed God," she admits. "I was getting along fine on my own."

As Teresa drifted further from the Church, she became more immersed in the beliefs of the secular culture. "I saw nothing wrong with sex outside of marriage. I saw nothing wrong with abortion. I pretty much accepted everything in the culture. But my main focus was on my future career and my goals. I wasn't concerned about what God wanted me to do; I was focused on what I wanted to do!"

What Does God Want?

When we think about God's will, there is a tendency to think in terms of something specific that God is asking us to do. But our first and foremost call from God is always a call to holiness.

This call to holiness is a movement in the soul that draws us toward a deeper union with God. We feel a growing desire to love God. We come to understand that there is a reason for our existence and that there is meaning in our lives. We begin to see that who we are in relation to God is more important than what we do.

> *The call to holiness is a process of ongoing conversion.*
> *It challenges us to trust God in the same way that a child*
> *trusts a loving parent. It encourages us to let go of our own*
> *selfish motives and desires. It invites us to embark on a*
> *spiritual journey that will deepen our faith, hope, and love.*
>
> *But the call to holiness is always a free choice. God*
> *never forces us to love Him. He extends invitations — and*
> *if we accept, we enter more deeply into the mystery of*
> *His love. If we refuse, God continues to nudge us, with the*
> *hope that we will someday respond.*

From age 9, Teresa had wanted a career in broadcasting. In 1981, her dream came true when she graduated from college with a degree in journalism and landed her first job at a local radio station. During this time, she met and married her husband, Dominic, an electrical engineer who had also been raised in a Catholic family. Like Teresa, Dominic had drifted away from the practice of the Catholic faith. They were married in a Catholic church, but their focus remained on their individual careers. They were both successful, and before long, they began to acquire "things." They dressed well, dined at expensive restaurants, and vacationed along what's known as Michigan's Gold Coast.

Trouble began five years later, when Teresa was offered a job in television. At first, it seemed like the perfect opportunity, but her job required her to do live reporting five nights a week. It meant that she would only see Dominic on weekends. Neither one of them saw it as a problem. They had no idea the toll this would take on their marriage.

Teresa became a rising star at the television station, and it was not unusual for her to put in extra hours. Increased responsibilities in Dominic's career required extra time spent at the office on weekends. "We rarely saw each other," she admits, "and when we did, it seemed that instead of trying to enjoy the little time we had together, we argued constantly."

What neither one of them recognized, however, was that the Holy Spirit was working to draw them back to each other and to God. The pivotal moment came with an invitation to a Detroit Pistons basketball game. During the game, a man sitting next to Dominic invited him to a men's Bible study. Dominic felt something stir inside of him, and he accepted the invitation. Those weekly sessions awakened in him a longing for God and the Catholic Church. He started to go to Mass again and enrolled in classes at Sacred Heart Major Seminary in Detroit. It was clear that Dominic had undergone a spiritual conversion.

What Is a Conversion?

A "conversion" can be defined as a specific event or a series of experiences that changes people's lives by opening them to new spiritual insights and a new sense of meaning or purpose in life. It can lead someone with "no faith" into believing in God. It can lead someone who already believes in God into a deeper dimension of belief and a more personal relationship with the Lord.

It's not uncommon for people undergoing a conversion to feel as if they are being spiritually drawn toward something. The reality is that God constantly pursues us, with the hope of drawing us closer to Himself. But we are always free to say yes or no to His gentle invitations.

Teresa felt threatened by her husband's new interest in religion, and she resented his attempts to bring her back to the Church. Angry and frustrated, she left Dominic and moved into a local hotel. She learned later that her faith-filled husband knelt down that night and asked the Lord to protect her. During his prayer, a sense of peace washed over him, and he felt certain that their marriage would be healed.

Several weeks later, Teresa moved back home. Dominic backed off on the religious pressure, but behind the scenes he prayed for her conversion. Teresa had to sink a little lower, however, before she could begin to climb her own spiritual ladder. The crash came when she was fired from the television station for no reason other than the management had decided to go in a different direction.

For six months, Teresa searched for another position. One day, on the edge of despair, she looked at a crucifix and prayed: *Okay, Lord, I know I've messed up.... Please come back into my life. I will do whatever is necessary and whatever You want. If You want me to stay home, that's fine. If You want me to still use my talents in the news business, that's fine too. Just take over, because I can't take this anymore!*

Afterward, Teresa remembers feeling an overwhelming sense of relief. She recommitted herself to her Catholic faith and resolved to seek help for her troubled marriage. Suddenly, she began to see the ways the Lord was speaking to her through the people around her. Her life began to change — and to her great surprise, she received a job offer at another local television station. Her husband encouraged her to take it as a sign that the Lord still wanted her in the secular media.

Teresa did not realize that this new job was not a final destination but rather another leg on her spiritual journey. She plunged back into her career — but at the same time, her spiritual life was drawing her in a different direction. She joined a women's Bible study. She and Dominic began counseling, and they attended a Marriage Encounter weekend that was offered in the Archdiocese of Detroit. They went on a pilgrimage to the Holy Land. They volunteered to help with the engaged-couples program in their parish.

Without realizing what was happening, Teresa's spiritual involvement began to affect the way she saw the world around her. She began to notice the sensationalism in the news and the media bias against religion. The thought occurred to her that God might be asking her to leave the secular media. Her first reaction was anger: *How could God put me back into a television station but now change His mind?*

When Teresa learned about an opening at a local radio station, she decided maybe this was the answer. For the next two years, it seemed as if radio was the perfect job for her. She was on the air in the early mornings and left the studio at noon, which gave her plenty of time to pursue her spiritual interests and nurture her marriage. But after a while, things began to change at the radio station. There was increased pressure to sensationalize the news and to increase what she calls "the sleaze factor," with off-color jokes and comments during the on-air programs.

"Over the course of this two-year stint, I went to great lengths to convince myself that I could keep one foot in the secular world and one foot in the Christian world," Teresa admits. "But I simply could not serve two masters. The industry had changed, and I had changed. Even though I tried to fit in, I no longer could. There was an unsettling feeling deep down that would not go away."

Secular *vs.* Spiritual

As people begin their journey back to God and the Catholic Church, they are sometimes confronted with glaring differences between the ways of the secular world and the ways of God. For example, consider these:

- **The secular world promotes materialism:** *"How much more can I get?" But the Lord urges us to simplify our lives and share what we have with those who are less fortunate.*
- **The secular world revolves around consumerism:** *"I make decisions based on what I see in advertisements and in the media." But the Lord tells us to base our decisions on the truth that has been revealed to us in Scripture and sacred Tradition.*
- **The secular world supports hedonism:** *"If it feels good, do it." But the Lord makes it clear that real happiness can be achieved only through moderation, self-discipline, and self-sacrifice.*
- **The secular world celebrates narcissism:** *"It's all about me!" But the Lord asks us to realign our priorities by loving God and loving our neighbor.*
- **The secular world encourages individualism:** *"I don't need anybody else, and I don't need to be part of any group." But the Lord draws us into community and promises that wherever two or more are gathered in His name, He will be present.*

- **The secular world advocates relativism:** *"There is no such thing as right and wrong, because everything depends on circumstances." But the Lord directs us to observe the laws of nature, morality, social responsibility, and the Church.*
- **The secular world promotes "victimism":** *"It's never my fault. I can always find someone to blame for my problems and mistakes." But the Lord tells us that we are personally accountable for what we say and do.*
- **The secular world embraces sensationalism:** *"I am intrigued by stories on the Internet and in the media that depict the basest behaviors in human nature." But the Lord calls us to lives of holiness and encourages us to model ourselves after the saints.*
- **The secular world wallows in nihilism:** *"Nothing has meaning." But the Lord assures us that there is meaning and purpose in this world, and He offers the promise of eternal life.*

After 20 years in broadcasting, Teresa came to the conclusion that, in good conscience, she could no longer do what the radio station wanted her to do. She explained to the station manager that she was no longer in sync with the direction that the station was taking. The manager agreed to buy out the remainder of her contract, and she used the money to start her own communications company.

Friends and colleagues thought she had lost her mind, but Dominic was supportive, and Teresa forged ahead with a website and the beginnings of a public-speaking career. She spoke to groups about media awareness and the negative influences of the entertainment ministry. She incorporated her own experiences into her talks, including the challenges she faced at age 12, when her attempts to emulate her favorite television star led to anorexia nervosa, which emaciated her body. She revealed what she had experienced with media bias, sensationalism, violence, and manipulation.

Before long, the program director at an evangelical radio station asked if she would like to do a talk show. "Unbeknownst to me, he was in the process of converting to Catholicism," she recalls. "I hosted *Christian Talk with Teresa Tomeo* at the evangelical station for two and a half years and then moved to Ave Maria Radio, where I was asked to host a program called *Catholic Connection.*"

Catholic Connection aired for the first time in December 2002. Three years later, it was picked up for national syndication through the EWTN Global Catholic Radio Network. Teresa Tomeo is now heard daily on more than 120 radio stations around the country, in addition to Sirius Satellite Radio and the Internet.

In 2007, Teresa's first book, *Noise: How Our Media-Saturated Culture Dominates Lives and Dismantles Families*, was published. Additional books have followed.

"What has happened to me can only have happened by the hand of God," Teresa acknowledges. "There is simply no other explanation. The pieces of the puzzle of my life continued to be lovingly placed by the hand of God. The pace of events that occurred at that time still takes my breath away. And it hasn't slowed down since!"

For Additional Information

- Teresa Tomeo, *Newsflash! My Surprising Journey from Secular Anchor to Media Evangelist* (Bezalel Books, 2008).
- Teresa Tomeo, Molly Miller, and Monica Cops, (All Things Girl series) *Truth for Teens; Girls Rock!; Friends, Boys, and Getting Along; Mirror, Mirror on the Wall, What Is Beauty After All?; Mind Your Manners; Modern and Modest; All Things Girl Journal* (Bezalel Books, 2008-2009).
- Teresa Tomeo, Molly Miller, and Monica Cops, *All Things Guy: A Guide to Becoming a Man that Matters* (Bezalel Books, 2009).
- Teresa Tomeo, *Noise: How Our Media-Saturated Culture Dominates Lives and Dismantles Families* (Ascension Press, 2007).

Websites

- Teresa Tomeo: *www.teresatomeo.com*
- *Catholic Connection*: *www.avemariaradio.net/christian-radio-host.php /Teresa-Tomeo*

Leo Severino

*Leo Severino is one of the founders of Metanoia Films,
which produced the award-winning movie* Bella. *He was in
his third year of law school when he reclaimed his
Catholic faith. He lives in Southern California
with his wife, Jacque, and their two children.*

Born on September 11, 1972, in Southern California, LEO
SEVERINO grew up in a Catholic family. "We were cultural
Catholics because my parents are from Colombia," he explains. "We went to Mass on Sunday, but I had no real interest in anything that was happening. It meant nothing to me.
The only thing I cared about was squeezing my brother's
hand really tight during the Our Father and being the first
to stand up and sit down during the Mass!"

By the time Leo entered college, he was no longer going
to Mass, and he describes himself as "a pretty solid pagan."

He had no relationship with God, and he lived by the philosophy that as long as he didn't hurt anybody else, he was morally okay.

"I was happy that way," Leo admits. "When your only standard is that you won't hurt anybody else, life is easy, because it means you have no standard. It's what Pope Benedict XVI calls the 'dictatorship of relativism.' "

What Is Relativism?

Relativism is based on the belief that there is no absolute truth and that all points of view are equally valid. This way of thinking puts all moral and ethical guidelines, all religious beliefs, and all philosophies at the whim of the individual, who ultimately decides what he or she wants to believe.

Then-Cardinal Joseph Ratzinger (the future Pope Benedict XVI) warned that relativism threatens to obscure universal truth about the nature of human beings, our purpose, and our destiny: "We are building a dictatorship of relativism that does not recognize anything as definitive and whose ultimate goal consists solely of one's own ego and desires" (April 18, 2005).

Leo's acceptance of relativism began to crumble during a philosophy class in college, in which he was exposed for the first time to St. Thomas Aquinas and the proofs of God's existence. He remembers thinking: *This could be true! Why don't more people know about this?*

A seed was planted in Leo's heart, but it didn't blossom until several years later when he was a law student. One afternoon he stopped at a bookstore in London. He noticed a book jutting out from the shelf. It was *The Problem of Pain*, by C. S. Lewis.

As a child, Leo had loved Lewis' *Chronicles of Narnia*, so he bought the book and read it cover to cover throughout the night. The book turned his whole world upside down. "I realized how much I was missing in my life," he admits. "I realized how much I had squandered and how much the Lord really meant to me. Amidst a lot of tears and repenting, my whole house of cards came tumbling down. It totally rocked my world, and it changed my life."

Leo started to read Catholic authors, including Hilaire Belloc, G. K. Chesterton, Frank Sheed, Archbishop Fulton Sheen, and Scott Hahn. By the time he graduated from law school in 1999, he had completely recommitted himself to the Catholic faith. He joined a parish in Irvine, California, attended Mass, and started volunteering in youth ministry. Teens flocked to him because he was young, interesting, and relevant in his approach to God and life. He eventually started his own youth group that explored Catholic beliefs. He called it "Going Deeper," and it quickly grew to more than 100 teens.

The biggest problem Leo faced, however, was how to align his legal career with his Catholic faith. He had been hired at Gibson, Dunn & Crutcher, one of the world's largest law firms, but after two years, he was not happy. During law school, he had spent the summer of 1997 working at 20th Century Fox, and he loved the excitement of the entertainment industry. He wanted to apply for a position in their legal department, but he feared that he would face ethical and moral conflicts. He remembers praying: *Lord, I* can't work in Hollywood unless You put me in a place where I can serve You.

The Power of Prayer

Sometimes people who have been away from the Church for a while struggle with prayer. One of the best ways to pray is to simply talk to God from the depths of your heart. Pour out your pain, fear, questions, and doubts. The essence of true prayer is giving oneself to God. Perhaps the best advice comes from St. Francis de Sales: "When you come before the Lord, talk to Him if you can; if you can't, just stay there, let yourself be seen, and don't try too hard to do anything else."

Leo felt that his prayer had been answered when he was offered a job as director of business affairs for the Fox Network Group. He accepted the position and became the youngest executive in the department. Ethics was not a problem because he worked on legal contracts for mostly innocuous programming. He believed his prayer had been answered.

Leo stayed at Fox for three years. When his contract was almost ready to be renewed, he began to attend daily Mass at Good Shepherd Parish in Beverly Hills, where he prayed for guidance in his life and his work. "I knew the Lord wanted me to do something different, but I wasn't sure what it was," he recalls.

After Mass one day, he saw another young man standing before a statue of the Sacred Heart with his hand raised in silent prayer. Leo walked by without saying anything, but he had the sense that he was supposed to talk to that young man.

Several weeks later, Leo saw the young man again. He decided to introduce himself, but he was interrupted by a woman who was seeking directions to a nearby restaurant. Twenty minutes passed while Leo talked to the woman. The young man was still praying in front of the statue, and Leo was already late for work, so he decided to leave without saying anything. "I figured this guy had incredible faith, or there was something wrong with him," he recalls.

When Leo finally got to the parking lot, his car was blocked by another car. He started to maneuver his vehicle out of the space so that he could leave by a different route. At that moment, the young man, who had been praying in church, walked by Leo's car. Leo rolled down the window and spoke to him. The young man introduced himself as Eduardo Verástegui and told Leo he was an actor. Leo asked why he was at Mass and was stunned to discover that Eduardo had also been seeking the Lord's guidance for his future. They shared a little bit of their stories of reclaiming their Catholic faith. Then they exchanged telephone numbers.

"He told me he was working on a film, but I didn't pay much attention to it," Leo admits. "When you're at Fox, everyone's an actor. I figured he was a bit player."

When Leo got back to the office, he checked Eduardo out on the Internet. He was shocked to learn that Eduardo was a television star and a member of a popular "boy band" in Mexico. He had been named one of the 100 most beautiful people in the world by *People* magazine. He was the Mexican equivalent of Brad Pitt, and he was in the process of crossing over into the United States' entertainment industry with the film *Chasing Papi*.

Leo called Eduardo to apologize for not recognizing him, and by the time the conversation ended, he had invited

Eduardo to attend his Going Deeper group. During the session, it became apparent that Eduardo knew very little about the Catholic faith, but he was eager to learn more. He suggested that Leo start a Going Deeper group in Hollywood for actors, directors, producers, and others in the film industry who were searching for God.

Unlike Leo, who had read his way back into the Catholic Church, Eduardo was drawn back to the Catholic Church in a completely different way. He had signed with a studio to play the role of a Latin lover who was dating three women at the same time. During rehearsals for the film, he was assigned an English-language coach named Jasmine O'Donnell. She was a devout Catholic, and she sensed something different about Eduardo. He seemed more sensitive and introspective than other young actors she had encountered who cared only about themselves and their careers.

Jasmine started to ask Eduardo questions about what he really wanted from life and whether the role of a Latin playboy, thief, drunk, and drug dealer fit the image that he wanted to project. She never preached or pushed. She just asked questions. Before long, Eduardo began to see that media images could have an impact on people, for good or for evil. It occurred to him that he had been using his God-given talents in a selfish way. He began to feel as if he had offended God by the way he had lived his life.

What Is the Purpose of Life?

The search for meaning and purpose in life is at the root of many people's decision to return to the Catholic faith. It's not unusual at some point in our lives to ask ourselves, "What is my purpose?" or "Is there meaning in my existence?"

As Catholics, we believe that our ultimate purpose in life is to use our God-given gifts and talents in ways that build the kingdom of God and carry on the mission of Jesus Christ. St. Teresa of Ávila reminds us: "Christ has no body now but yours. Yours are the eyes through which He is to go about doing good. Yours are the hands with which He is to bless people now."

We are all called to be part of God's divine plan. But we have also been given a free will that allows us to disregard the movement of the Holy Spirit in our lives. Our true purpose in life is clear — and once we recognize it, we have a choice as to whether or not we want to pursue it.

Eduardo decided to never again accept a role that would be offensive to God. He considered leaving Hollywood entirely so that he could do missionary work in Brazil, but a priest assured him that God had bigger plans for him in Hollywood. Eduardo started to attend Mass every day at Good Shepherd Parish to ask for God's guidance. It was there that he met Leo.

Not long after their meeting, Eduardo told Leo that he wanted to start a movie-production company that would produce movies without violence, crime, and exploitation. He asked Leo to be his manager, attorney, and agent. Then Eduardo told Leo about his friend Alejandro Monteverde, an award-winning young director who had graduated from the University of Texas film school and was on a similar spiritual path. Eduardo envisioned the three of them working together as a team.

A short time later, the three men met at Good Shepherd for Mass and then went to Eduardo's home, where they sat around a coffee table and formed a new production company. Eduardo wanted to call the company "Metanoia Films," which comes from the Greek word for "conversion," because he realized that conversion was what he was going through. Leo saw another meaning for the word "conversion," which is "turning from the darkness to the light," and he points out that this is precisely the effect that they had hoped their films would have on viewers.

"We knew that everything, including Hollywood, belonged to God," Leo explains, "and we wanted to try and claim Hollywood back for God. That might seem crazy and idealistic, but we didn't care because we knew it was true."

They took as their mission statement a quote from Mother Teresa in which she said, "We are not called to be successful. We are called to be faithful."

Blessed Mother Teresa of Calcutta

Mother Teresa never left the Catholic Church, but she did experience a profound midlife conversion that changed the course of her life. She was on a train heading for a spiritual retreat in the mountains when she heard what she described as "a call within a call" to leave the convent and work directly with the poor and dying in the streets of Calcutta. By responding to that call, she changed the course of her own life, and she influenced the lives of millions of people who have been inspired by her work.

Over the next few weeks, Leo, Eduardo, and Alejandro read scripts, but they kept rejecting the stories because they were not in keeping with their goal of making a movie that would touch people's lives in a positive way.

Finally, Alejandro told them about an idea he had for a film. The story had come to him while he was driving from Texas to Los Angeles. He was thinking about two people he knew, and he began to imagine what might happen if they ever met. Scenes began to flash through his mind: *What if she were pregnant and thinking about an abortion? What if he were the only friend that she had, the only one who would listen, the only one who could share her pain, her confusion, her fears?* Several times Alejandro had to pull off the road because tears clouded his vision. By the time he reached Los Angeles, the story had formed in his mind.

Leo and Eduardo listened as the plot unfolded, and they both realized that this story could make a difference in today's world. It was exactly the kind of film that they wanted to produce. Before long, everything started to fall into place. They secured funding for the project before they even had a finished script. Eduardo would play the male lead. They found the perfect actress, Tammy Blanchard, for the female lead. The name of the movie was simply *Bella*, which means "beautiful." There was never any doubt in their minds that the Lord was orchestrating everything.

They shot the film in New York City. The Franciscan Friars of the Renewal invited Leo, Eduardo, and some other members of the cast and crew to live at their monastery during the filming. The friars supported the effort with their prayers, and Leo was convinced that they were seeing minor miracles unfold on a daily basis. Perhaps the greatest miracle of all was that they stayed within their $3 million budget and that they completed filming on schedule.

When the movie was finished, they had to figure out how to get it into theaters. "We knew that film festivals were where the distributors were, and they are the best places to promote a movie since all of the press attends also," Leo explains.

They decided to submit *Bella* to the 2006 Toronto International Film Festival. Their chances of having the film accepted were slim, because only 300 movies are actually chosen from more than 6,000 submissions. But there was something special about *Bella*. The codirector of the festival called Leo to tell him that she loved *Bella* so much that she had asked twelve people to review it. Ten of the twelve loved it, and the other two thought it was good. As a result, *Bella* was not only chosen as one of the films that would be shown at the festival, but this woman had also listed it as one of the top ten picks. By opening night, the tickets for *Bella* had already sold out.

No one expected *Bella* to win an award, however, because it was competing against high-budget movies like *All the King's Men*, *Death of a President*, *Babel*, *Bobby*, and *Departed*. "We felt like very little fish swimming in a huge pond," Leo recalls.

When the announcement was made that *Bella* had won the People's Choice Award, the top prize at the Toronto Film Festival, everyone was stunned. It wasn't long before more awards came. Over 300 U.S. organizations endorsed the film, and nearly 170 coalitions were forged with Latino groups, church groups, pro-life organizations, and the adoption community. When *Bella* was finally released in U.S. theaters in October 2007, it grossed over $1.3 million on the first weekend and over $12 million worldwide. The response to the film was so great that it remained in some theaters for 26 weeks. The DVD was released in May 2008.

"The most beautiful surprises are the things people get out of the film that we didn't anticipate them getting," Leo explains. "That confirmed to us that anything the Lord touches is like a diadem. Whatever lives are touched, it's going to be reflecting different colors to different people where they're standing."

During the making of *Bella*, Alejandro met his future wife at a Going Deeper session that Leo was conducting in Hollywood. During this time, Leo also fell in love with the woman with whom he was destined to spend the rest of his life. Leo and Jacque were married on July 7, 2007. In 2008, their first child, Mina Marie, was born. Their son, Lukas, was born in 2010.

Reports of other babies that were born because the parents were inspired by the movie *Bella* began to pour in. "There are a lot of stories — in short, where people watch the film, not knowing what it is about, having already scheduled an abortion, but after seeing the movie, decide not to abort their child," Leo explains.

In the future, Metanoia Films hopes to continue making entertaining movies that will carry a solid faith message to a broader audience in a nonjudgmental, loving, and effective way. Leo has also continued his Going Deeper discussions, which take place once a month on Wednesday evenings at Family Theater, on Sunset Boulevard in Hollywood.

"It's so inspiring to wake up in the morning and know that you're working for something you really believe in," Leo says. "It's addictive in the best possible sense — personally, spiritually, and in all other ways. I'm inspired to keep going on this mission."

For Additional Information

- Tim Drake, *Behind Bella: The Amazing Stories of Bella and the Lives It's Changed* (Ignatius Press, 2008).
- C. S. Lewis, *The Problem of Pain* (Touchstone, 1996).

Websites

- *Bella: www.bellamoviesite.com*
- Going Deeper: *www.goingdeeperdiscussions.com*

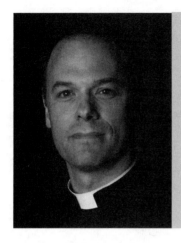

Father John Fletcher, C.C.

Father Fletcher is a member of the Companions of the Cross, a Catholic community of priests called to the ongoing renewal of the Church through evangelization in the wisdom and power of the Holy Spirit. They proclaim the Good News of Jesus Christ to the people they are called to serve, with special attention to parish communities, the poor, youths, and those alienated from the Church.

JOHN FLETCHER was born in March 1964 in Williamsville, New York, and grew up in a Catholic family. "We went to church every Sunday like all good Catholics," he recalls. "We prayed before every meal and before anyone went on a trip. Each night before bed, my mother would remind us to say our prayers. In fact, my mother was always ready to pray about any need we might have, especially if someone was sick or hurt."

John's father was more pragmatic. If he couldn't see it or touch it, he didn't really believe it, and he didn't always go to Mass with the family. "He would come to church with us because he was supposed to," Father Fletcher recalls. "It wasn't until later in life that my father grew quite close to the Lord."

One of Father Fletcher's earliest memories is when he was only 3 or 4 years old. His mother was helping him get dressed when his sister came in the room and asked if their mother was planning to bring John to "c-h-u-r-c-h." "She spelled the word, and even though I didn't know how to spell, I figured it out and started screaming that I was not going to church!" he admits.

John's dislike of going to Mass intensified as he got older. His mother recalls dragging him out of bed by the legs one Sunday morning. Angry and frustrated, she sought the advice of an archbishop, who happened to be a friend of the family, on how to deal with her son. Archbishop Joseph Raya suggested that she knock on John's door and politely invite him to come to Mass, instead of trying to force him. "If he doesn't want to go, then go to Mass with the rest of the family, and don't get angry!" he advised.

His mother's new attitude took the pressure off. John started to come to Mass occasionally, but while he was there, he bided his time by counting ceiling tiles and windows. "Sometimes I would pretend there was a typewriter on my lap, and I would practice typing things that I heard during Mass — anything to pass the time!"

Another Look at the Mass

It's not unusual for people to complain that the Mass is boring. When people begin to think in those terms, it is usually because they don't understand what is happening and how they can enter into the sacred mysteries that are taking place.

When you come to Mass, you have the opportunity to pray with your whole being. You have the opportunity to do the following:

- *Seek forgiveness for your sins.*
- *Listen as God speaks to you in the readings, the music, and the homily.*
- *Offer yourself to the Lord.*
- *Experience the miracle of bread and wine changing into the Body and Blood of Christ.*
- *Reach out to others in a sign of peace.*
- *Receive the Body, Blood, Soul, and Divinity of Christ.*
- *Go forth with the mandate to carry the love and peace of Christ into the world.*

The Mass was never intended to be entertaining. It is a ritual in which people move beyond feelings into authentic prayer, which is the offering of oneself to God in Jesus Christ.

Father Fletcher also recalls that as a young teenager, he went through a period in which he was angry at God. He was in the eighth grade, and his friends were making fun of him because he refused to smoke pot. He stopped hanging around with them and blamed God for allowing him to be so unhappy. One Easter, during the renewal of baptismal vows, when the congregation was asked if they believed in the basic tenets of the Catholic faith, everyone responded, "I do," except for John, who stubbornly insisted, "I don't!"

By high school, John had made new friends, and he was no longer being belligerent toward God, but he still did not like going to Mass. By the time he entered college, he rarely went to church on his own. None of his friends had any real spirituality. Religion was just not part of their lives.

After college, John moved to California, and he would go to Mass occasionally with his two brothers, Hal and Steve. Hal had gone through a conversion several years earlier. John did not pay much attention to Hal's religious insights or experiences until Hal told him about an atheist friend who was dying. Hal tried to tell her about Jesus and life after death, but she was not interested. A short time later, she slipped into a coma for three days, and when she awoke, she told Hal that while she was in the coma, she had been with Jesus twice. She became a believer, and she embraced her approaching death with deep peace and serenity.

"This story had an enormous effect on me," Father Fletcher recalls. "I remember specifically thinking that this was the kind of story I could easily dismiss as a sick person's delirium, but I chose to believe it, and I have never had the slightest doubt about it since."

Still, John struggled with other doubts and uncertainties. "I had a fair amount of trouble understanding the relationship between Jesus and God the Father," he explains. "I felt that if God created everything, He must have created Jesus, so why should we pray to Jesus instead of God? But after the story that Hal told about his friend, I started to believe that Jesus was real."

Hal encouraged John to read C. S. Lewis' *The Great Divorce*, which is an allegory about heaven and hell. It answered some of John's questions about what happens to the soul when someone dies. "The big thing I got out of this book was that we all have the opportunity to commit ourselves to loving and accepting God totally," he recalls. "Of course, we also have the chance to refuse this, and in so doing, we choose hell. This made perfect sense to me. I figured I would have no problem getting into heaven if I just decided to love and accept God."

Apart from these new insights, John's life was really no different than before. He went to Mass only when his brothers asked him to go. "I spent no more time thinking about Jesus than before," he admits. "I was still doing whatever I wanted and did not feel that I needed to change anything."

His next turning point was prompted by his other brother, Steve, who told him about a friend who had experienced a vision of Our Lady. John was curious but not convinced. Steve gave him a rosary and suggested that he use it. "Well, that night I started to pray the Rosary in bed," he recalls. "I found that it was not as difficult or tedious as I thought it might be, and I kept at it pretty much every night after that. I had no way of knowing it, but by making the decision to pray the Rosary, I had ever so slightly cracked open the door to my heart, and God stuck His foot in before I could close it again!"

All of this was taking place in the mid-1990s, at which time John attended a lecture by someone who claimed that the Blessed Virgin was appearing to people all over the world, telling us that God exists, that He is displeased with our behavior, and that He wants us to repent and turn back to Him. John ended up reading the speaker's book, which explored the phenomenon of Marian apparitions. John was especially moved by the reports of many miracles taking place in Medjugorje, and he learned about a shrine near Denver where apparitions had been reported. With that in mind, John decided to visit Denver and see things for himself.

What Catholics Believe About Marian Apparitions

Marian apparitions are considered private revelations. The Church has declared that some apparitions — such as Our Lady's appearances in Guadalupe, Mexico (1531), Lourdes, France (1858), and Fátima, Portugal (1917) — are "worthy of belief." But the Church does not require belief in any apparition.

During the past hundred years, there have been 386 claims of Marian apparitions. According to the International Marian Research Institute at the University of Dayton, the Church has reached "no decision" in most of the cases. Seventy-nine cases were dismissed. Only nine cases have been approved

The Church is cautious about apparitions because Jesus Himself derided those who seek out the extraordinary: "An evil and adulterous generation seeks for a sign" (Matthew 16:4).

Jesus also warned against false messiahs and false prophets, who "will arise and show great signs and wonders, so as to lead astray, if possible, even the elect" (Matthew 24:24).

The appropriate Catholic response to apparitions should not center on curiosity or sensationalism but rather on an increase of faith, and an attitude of thanksgiving and praise for the goodness of God.

When Hal learned of John's desire to go to Denver, he told John that it would be good for him to prepare spiritually. Part of this preparation meant going to confession, and on March 16, 1994, John went to confession for the first time in 20 years. He soon began attending daily Mass as well. "The door to my heart was opening wider and wider," he reveals.

A short time later, Hal invited John to attend a prayer meeting, and when they walked in the room, Hal introduced him as his brother, John, who was going to become a priest!

"Not me!" John retorted. John assumed Hal was joking, but Hal really believed that John had a vocation and just wasn't aware of it yet.

Having spent a few days praying at the shrine in Denver, John was a little disappointed that he didn't notice anything particularly special about this place. He mentioned it to someone he met on the trip, and his new friend told him that the reason for going on a pilgrimage was to pray and to get closer to God, not to look for supernatural phenomena. The friend assured John that he would receive graces just by being there, but he might not know about them for quite some time.

What Is Grace?

The Catechism of the Catholic Church *(CCC) tells us, "Grace is a* participation in the life of God*" (n. 1997, emphasis in original). Chances are you've experienced "graced" moments in your life. Maybe you felt as if you were in the presence of God. Maybe you realized that God was leading you, guiding you, or sustaining you.

These "graced" moments are the subtle ways God works in our lives to strengthen our faith and to invite us to follow His will.

While John was in Denver, he prayed the Way of the Cross for the first time in his life, and his eyes filled with tears as he contemplated how his sins had caused so much suffering to Jesus and to Mary, who watched her divine son die on the cross. Later that night, John joined all the people in the church in consecrating themselves to Jesus through Mary.

On his last night in Denver, John tried to figure out whether he had received any graces during the pilgrimage. He suspected that all along he had been undergoing a gradual conversion, but this night would be a real turning point for him.

"After a few minutes of quiet contemplation, I felt a sensation in my heart that began to spread all throughout my body," he explains. "This sensation took the form of an intense love for Jesus and Mary that had never been there before. It was an all-consuming feeling. If anyone would have asked me if I loved Jesus a few days earlier, I would have said, 'Probably not.' And if they asked about Mary, I would have said, 'What about her?' Now I felt a burning love for both of them. Along with the love, I also felt that I knew Jesus and Mary. It was the same way you know a friend. It was as if I knew them and had spent time with them. How did that happen? Not by anything I did, except being open to God. It was a grace given to me."

When John returned from Denver, he seemed like a different person, and people started asking him if he planned to become a priest. He continued going to daily Mass and joined three different prayer groups. He prayed the Rosary and the Chaplet of Divine Mercy. He went to confession weekly and renewed his consecration to Our Lady every three or four months. He read spiritual books, attended Marian conferences, and started working part-time in youth ministry.

It was during this time that John met a Vietnamese nun, who insisted that he should become a priest. When she found out that he was planning a trip to Medjugorje, she felt certain that he would recognize his vocation while he was there.

"I told her that it would take a huge neon sign in the sky from God telling me He wanted me to be a priest before I would ever do something like that," Father Fletcher recalls. "When I got back from Medjugorje and told her there had been no signs, she relented and said that maybe I wasn't meant to be a priest."

But John noticed other changes in his life when he returned from Medjugorje. He felt increasingly dissatisfied with his job, but he procrastinated about sending out résumés to look for a new job. It became more difficult for him to be around some of his old friends because they didn't share his new spirituality.

When someone let John borrow a magazine about religious vocations, the first article he read had a profound impact on him. "The person writing the article said that at a certain point in her life, she needed to be surrounded by people who were constantly seeking the face of God because she couldn't do it on her own," he recalls. "When I read that, it was like a lightbulb lit up in my head. It was exactly what I was feeling. I needed the support of others who were seeking closeness with God."

It wasn't until a few months later that he began to seriously think about the priesthood. A friend was going to Canada to check out a religious community called "Companions of the Cross." John decided to go with him, and he spent four days there asking all kinds of questions. Then he visited another religious community in Canada called "Madonna House."

"I kept asking God what He wanted me to do," Father Fletcher recalls. "He kept telling me over and over again to trust Him. Finally, after a year of asking what God's plan for my life was and after much prayer and consultation, I was feeling very exasperated and thought: *Okay, God, if You want trust, I'll give You trust. I can't tell if You want me to be a priest or not, but I'm willing to take the chance that You do. If that's what You want, then clear any obstacles, and give me peace every step of the way. If You don't want me to be a priest, then You'd better block my efforts.* I was really putting it on the line with God. But as soon as I made this declaration, I felt so much relief. The decision was no longer on my shoulders. I gave it to God to work out."

John eventually decided to enter into formation with the Companions of the Cross. He was ordained to the priesthood in June 2001. Since then, he has served as a university chaplain and the pastor of three parishes. In 2009, he began studies for a licentiate in sacred theology with a specialization in Mariology. Father Fletcher offers the following advice to anyone who may be thinking about coming back to the Catholic faith:

If you have even the slightest inkling about returning to the Church, be assured that this is a prompting of the Holy Spirit. Open your heart to God, and beg Him to guide you and to give you the courage to say yes to His promptings. Ask Him for the grace to make the decision to forgive whoever may have hurt you and to no longer let that be the excuse for being away from your faith. Outside of the Church, away from your faith, you are like a sheep that has wandered away from the protection of the shepherd. Jesus is the Good Shepherd, who dearly desires to care for us, and He gave us the Church to help provide that care.

For Additional Information

- C. S. Lewis, *The Great Divorce* (HarperOne, 2001).
- Catherine M. Odell, *Those Who Saw Her: Apparitions of Mary, Revised & Updated* (Our Sunday Visitor, 2010).
- Fulton J. Sheen, *The Way of the Cross* (Alba House, 2006).

Websites

- Companions of the Cross: *www.companionscross.org*
- The Marian Library/International Marian Research Institute at the University of Dayton: *http://campus.udayton.edu/mary/*

Veronica
Cavan

Veronica Cavan is one of the coordinators of Annulment
Companions in the Diocese of Buffalo. She came back to the
Church when her son was making his First Communion.
She and her husband, Ed, live in Amherst, New York. They
have three grown children.

VERONICA CAVAN was born into an Irish-American family
on March 31, 1950. She grew up in New York City, and
after attending a Catholic elementary and high school, she
enrolled at the City University of New York.

"It was quite a culture shock!" she recalls. "I was a mi-
nority for the first time in my life. I was a token Irish Catholic in a school that was predominantly Jewish."

Veronica loved college. It was an escape from her chaotic family life. She grew up in the Borough of Queens
with her parents, her two older brothers, her uncle, and her

grandmother — all living in the same small apartment. "We had a lot of love in our family, but we yelled a lot," she recalls. "In my family, if you did anything wrong, you heard about it forever!"

Veronica's older brothers were both married by the time she was a sophomore in high school. Her grandmother had died several years earlier. Her mother suffered from depression, and after Veronica's father passed away during her sophomore year in college, her mother became very dependent on her. Veronica remembers how people at her father's funeral would say to her mother, "At least you have Veronica to take care of you." Veronica felt trapped.

When she was a senior in college, she met her future husband. It was the first serious relationship she had ever had. "His family was everything my family was not," Veronica admits. He was Jewish, but his family never went to religious services; her family went to Mass every week. His family had a lot of money and a big house on Long Island; her family lived in a five-room apartment in Queens.

When they decided to get married, neither family was happy about it. Her fiancé was planning to go on for a doctorate in history at the University of Buffalo, which meant that Veronica would have to move upstate and work as a teacher to support both of them while he went to graduate school.

Veronica wanted to get married in a Catholic church. His mother insisted that if she ever had to walk into a Catholic church, she would have a heart attack. Veronica's mother said if she didn't get married in a Catholic church, she was going to go to hell! They broke up several times during their engagement, but they always got back together.

"In my mind, marriage was an opportunity to be independent," she explains. "I grew up in a family where a daughter didn't leave home unless she left in a wedding dress!"

They finally decided to get married in a nonsectarian chapel at the United Nations. Veronica obtained all of the proper permissions and dispensations from the Catholic Church, and her brother called it a three-ring circus because a Catholic priest, a Jewish rabbi, and the nondenominational minister from the chapel officiated. The minister was actually the one who signed the marriage certificate, but they didn't tell either side of the family.

They settled in Buffalo, New York, but things did not go well from the very start. They argued a lot. Veronica was earning the money, and her husband was spending it. He discouraged her from joining a parish and going to Mass. When she brought up the subject of children, he told her that he didn't want to have children.

Veronica began to feel isolated. Her husband didn't like her family or her friends. He only wanted to socialize with his friends. She later discovered that he had been carrying on an affair during his frequent "research" trips. He eventually admitted that he did not want to be married anymore, and after four years of a chaotic relationship, they were divorced.

A short time later, Veronica met the love of her life. She inquired about the possibility of a Church annulment but was told that she was married to her first husband for life and that there was nothing she could do about it. So Veronica and Ed Cavan were married by a Protestant minister in 1976.

Ed had been raised with no religion, and when Veronica told him that she wanted to raise their children as Catholics, he had no objection. She arranged for each of their three children to be baptized as infants — and when her youngest was baptized, she admitted to the priest that she didn't go to Mass because she couldn't receive Communion. He suggested that she look into the possibility of an annulment. He told her that canon law had been revised in 1983 and that new grounds for annulment were now possible. The priest even gave her the paperwork. She looked it over but decided not to do anything about it. She felt as if she had been rejected once by the Church, and she was apprehensive about being rejected again.

What the Church Believes About Divorce and Annulment

The Catholic Church holds to the basic teachings of Jesus that prohibit divorce and remarriage (Matthew 5:31-32, Mark 10:11-12, Luke 16:18). The Church defines marriage as a " 'covenant, by which a man and a woman establish between themselves a partnership of the whole of life' (CIC, can. 1055 § 1; cf. GS 48 § 1)" (CCC, 1601). The Catholic Church recognizes marriage as a sacrament and teaches that a valid sacramental marriage is indissoluble except by the death of one spouse.

However, not every couple that marries actually forms a sacramental bond at the time the marriage vows are exchanged, because of immaturity, psychological problems, lack of honesty, or no real commitment on the part of one or both parties. For this reason, the Church has an annulment process to examine whether a marriage was truly valid.

If you are divorced and remarried outside the Catholic Church, it might be a good idea to talk to a priest or someone at the diocesan marriage tribunal about the circumstances in your marriage. You might have grounds for an annulment.

When Veronica's son reached school age, she enrolled him in religious-education classes that were held on Sunday mornings. "I know that you really want to go back to church yourself," her husband told her. "It's okay. I'll go with you."

So they started going to Mass as a family, but none of them could receive Communion, and Veronica admits that she really didn't feel as if she belonged there.

When her son was ready to make his First Communion, Veronica went to the parents meeting. All of the other parents seemed to know one another, but no one talked to her. She sat alone, and she started to think she had made a mistake in coming when the director of religious education asked if she would help. The children were lining up to practice receiving Communion. The director led Veronica to the main aisle and gave her a ciborium filled with unconsecrated hosts. She told Veronica to say, "Body of Christ," as she placed a host in each child's hand.

Veronica's face flushed with embarrassment. She couldn't receive Communion herself because of her marital status, but she didn't want to explain in front of all those people why she shouldn't be doing this.

"So I stood there," she recalls, "and as I repeated the words 'Body of Christ'... 'Body of Christ'... 'Body of Christ,' I felt an intense hunger for the Eucharist. I was overwhelmed with the presence of God. My whole body trembled. It was like nothing I had ever experienced before. It was as if God were saying to me, 'I'm here. I never walked away from you.'"

In the weeks that followed, little things started happening. Veronica would notice something in the bulletin about annulments, or someone would say something that touched her heart. "I really believed that it was God calling me."

She ordered a book about annulments and went to an annulment workshop sponsored by the diocese. Then she sat down and in one evening completed the paperwork for the marriage tribunal.

By the time her second child was ready to make her First Communion, Veronica had received her annulment, and her marriage to Ed was convalidated during a private ceremony at her parish. "I was not prepared for how powerful it would be when our marriage was blessed," she admits. "It was for my husband as well."

Having a Marriage Blessed

After receiving an annulment from the Church, two people who were married earlier outside the Church can arrange to have their marriage blessed by a priest or deacon. The ceremony is called "convalidation." Arrangements are made through the parish priest or deacon. Some couples arrange for a simple ceremony with just two witnesses present. Others opt for a formal ceremony with a Mass and invited guests.

When Veronica's third child was preparing for First Communion, her husband, Ed, decided to become a Catholic. He joked that he didn't want to be the only one in the pew who couldn't receive Communion. But what really happened was that he had listened to what his children were learning, and he, too, wanted to receive the Body and Blood of Christ.

"The annulment process was healing for me," Veronica explains. "It helped me find closure, and it brought me back to the Church."

Today, Veronica and Ed are both actively involved in parish ministries and events. Veronica was also instrumental in organizing a new ministry in her diocese called "Annulment Companions." She uses her own annulment experience, along with her giftedness as a teacher, to offer support and encouragement to people who are seeking annulments.

The Facts About Divorce and Annulment

There are many misconceptions about divorce and annulment. Here are the facts:

- Someone who is divorced is not automatically excommunicated.
- A divorced person is not required to obtain an annulment unless he or she would like to remarry in a Catholic ceremony.
- An annulment is a declaration by the Catholic Church that when the marriage vows were exchanged, there was an impediment that prevented one or both partners from making a mature, lifelong commitment.
- An annulment does not make children illegitimate.
- An annulment does not cost thousands of dollars.

- *An annulment can be granted even if one of the ex-spouses refuses to cooperate.*
- *The annulment process does not focus on the reasons the marriage ended. It looks at factors that influenced the couple leading up to the wedding. It is a soul-searching process that involves prayer, reflection, and spiritual insights.*

For Additional Information

- Lorene Hanley Duquin, *Seeking an Annulment with the Help of Your Catholic Faith* (Our Sunday Visitor, 2007).
- Edward N. Peters, J.D., J.C.D., *Annulments and the Catholic Church: Straight Answers to Tough Questions* (Ascension Press, 2004).

Websites

- DivorcedCatholic.org: *www.divorcedcatholic.com*
- North American Conference of Separated and Divorced Catholics: *www.nacsdc.org*
- BeginningCatholic.com/Catholic Annulment: Was a Marriage Valid?: *www.beginningcatholic.com/catholic-annulment.html*
- EWTN/Annulment/Decree of Nullity: *www.ewtn.com/expert/answers /annulment.htm*

For additional information and copies of annulment forms, check your diocesan website, or call your diocesan marriage tribunal.

Clarence Thomas

Clarence Thomas is an associate justice of the Supreme
Court of the United States. He returned to
the Catholic faith in 1996.

CLARENCE THOMAS, a descendant of West African slaves,
was born in Pin Point, Georgia, on June 23, 1948.* He was
the middle child in the family, with one older sister and
one younger brother. His parents divorced, and his father

---

* The information in this profile was obtained from the following sources:
Clarence Thomas, *My Grandfather's Son: A Memoir* (HarperCollins,
2007); Kevin Merida and Michael A. Fletcher, *Supreme Discomfort: The
Divided Soul of Clarence Thomas* (Doubleday, 2007); Ken Foskett, *Judging
Thomas: The Life and Times of Clarence Thomas* (HarperCollins, 2004);
Andrew Peyton Thomas, *Clarence Thomas: A Biography* (Encounter
Books, 2001).

abandoned the family when Clarence was only 2 years old. They lived with his mother's aunt. "Nothing about my childhood seemed unusual to me at the time," he recalls. "I had no idea that any other life was possible, at least for me."

Everything changed after his aunt's house burned to the ground. His mother left her daughter in Pin Point and took her two little boys to Savannah, where she worked as a domestic earning 10 dollars a week. They lived in a tenement apartment with an outdoor toilet. Clarence slept on a chair and attended a public school for black children. He remembers "hunger without the prospect of eating and cold without the prospect of warmth."

The following year his mother made arrangements for Clarence and his brother to live with their grandparents, who owned a new cinder-block house with two bedrooms, a living room, dining room, kitchen, den, and indoor bathroom on East 32nd Street in Savannah. To Clarence it seemed like luxury. His grandfather made it clear, however, that if they were going to stay there, they would abide by his rules, regulations, manners, and good behavior. It wasn't long before Clarence began to call his grandfather "Daddy," and he thought of himself as his grandfather's son.

Most of the members of Clarence's extended family were Baptist. However, the nuns at a local Catholic parish had taught his grandfather to read, and in 1949 his grandfather had converted to Catholicism because he liked the Catholic rituals and discipline. He also believed that children behaved better when they wore uniforms, so he enrolled Clarence and his brother in a Catholic school for black children run by the Missionary Franciscan Sisters of the Immaculate Conception.

His grandfather also took Clarence and his brother to Mass every Sunday at St. Benedict the Moor, the first black Catholic parish in Georgia. Clarence received his First Communion, and when he was in the third grade, he became an altar boy. He made frequent visits to a local monastery, where a priest helped him to learn Latin.

After graduating from grammar school, Clarence entered St. Pius X, the only Catholic high school for blacks in Savannah. He was a good student and thought about becoming a priest. He hoped for some divine revelation that would make it clear whether he had a vocation. In 1964, he attended a diocesan convocation for altar boys, and afterward he told his grandfather that he wanted to transfer to the minor seminary to finish high school. His grandfather agreed, on one condition: "If you go, you have to stay. You can't quit."

Clarence was one of only two black students who had been admitted to the minor seminary. He felt as if he had landed in another world — an all-white world — where he was surrounded by "a sea of strange white faces." He remembers feeling constantly anxious and insecure. His day was rigidly structured with little free time. Classes were difficult, and there was a lot of homework, but he did well. When the racial prejudices of the other students revealed themselves in things that they said or did, Clarence found comfort praying before the Blessed Sacrament in the chapel. He persevered and graduated with outstanding grades. The faculty recommended that he continue his studies for the priesthood.

In 1967, Clarence entered Immaculate Conception Seminary in Missouri. It was a time of unrest — the civil rights movement, the Vietnam War, and the changes in the Church that had been sparked by the Second Vatican Council.

During that time, Clarence and another black seminarian both reeled from episodes of discrimination. They began to admit to each other their frustration at the way the Catholic Church treated blacks. Clarence became more uncertain of his vocation. During the Christmas break, he talked to a priest in Savannah who encouraged him to return to Immaculate Conception for another semester to determine whether he really had a calling to the priesthood.

Clarence went back to the seminary for the spring semester. In April, Clarence was walking into the dormitory when someone shouted the news that Dr. Martin Luther King, Jr., had been shot. Another seminarian replied, "That's good. I hope the son of a bitch dies." For Clarence, the hate-filled comment was a confirmation that he did not have a vocation.

The Sin of Racism

There is a long history of racism, prejudice, and discrimination against African Americans in the United States, which unfortunately included the Catholic Church. Discrimination and segregation were present in Catholic parishes, Catholic schools, and Catholic hospitals.

By the mid-1950s, several bishops condemned discrimination and made it clear that segregation in Catholic institutions would not be tolerated in their dioceses. In 1958, the American Catholic bishops issued "Discrimination and Christian Conscience," a pastoral letter stating that "the heart of the race question is moral and religious."

> By the 1960s, the Catholic bishops offered their support to the civil rights movement. Many Catholic priests, religious, and lay people participated in marches and demonstrations that advocated an end to discrimination and segregation. Efforts increased in Catholic parishes to put an end to racial prejudice.
>
> In 1979, the United States bishops issued "Brothers and Sisters to Us," a strongly worded pastoral letter on racism. In it they declared: "Racism is a sin: a sin that divides the human family, blots out the image of God among specific members of that family, and violates the fundamental human dignity of those called to be children of the same Father."
>
> The bishops also made it clear that every Catholic must acknowledge his or her role in the sinful attitudes and behaviors of the past that resulted in racism and prejudice. They asked parents to teach their children about respect for all. They instructed all Catholics to end racial stereotypes, racial slurs, and racial jokes.

Clarence's grandfather was devastated when he learned of Clarence's decision to leave the seminary. The next day, he told Clarence that he was no longer welcome in his home. He predicted that Clarence would end up a failure, and he made it clear that even if Clarence enrolled in another college, he would not help him with the tuition or expenses.

Clarence found a summer job and lived with his mother. He feared that he would never break through the wall of segregation, and he felt anger rise within him. He began to cast off the beliefs he had learned from his grandfather, the nuns, and the Catholic Church.

A friend, who was attending Holy Cross College in Massachusetts, urged Clarence to apply. He was accepted, with the assurance that tuition costs could be worked out. He was one of 6 black students in a class of 550. "During my second week on campus, I went to Mass for the first and last time at Holy Cross," he recalls. "I don't know why I bothered — probably habit, or guilt — but whatever the reason, I got up and walked out midway through the homily."

While Clarence was at Holy Cross, he met his future wife. They were engaged during his junior year and planned to marry the day after he graduated. As the wedding day neared, Clarence was filled with doubts. He wondered if he was too young. He stayed up the night before the ceremony getting drunk, and he showed up at the church the next day with a hangover. He recalls that "a bolt of sharp, sickening pain shot through my body as we said our vows.... I really didn't know whether I was doing the right thing. For one crazy moment, I thought of stopping the ceremony, but I knew it was too late to turn back."

That fall, Clarence entered Yale Law School. His wife worked as a teller to support them. In 1973, she gave birth to their first child. The following year, Clarence graduated from law school and accepted a position in the office of Missouri Attorney General John Danforth. Three years later, when Danforth was elected to the U.S. Senate, Clarence Thomas moved to a corporate law firm, but he later admitted that it was a mistake. He was not challenged by the work, and his personal life began to deteriorate. He felt increasingly unhappy in his marriage. He had severed his ties with the Catholic Church, and feelings of hopelessness led him to drink as a way to ease the pain.

In 1979, an invitation from Senator Danforth to work for him in Washington as a legislative aide offered a glimmer of hope. His professional life soared, but his personal life remained troublesome, and he hated himself for his inability to be a loving husband.

Two years later, Clarence went to work in the Reagan administration as assistant secretary of education for the Office of Civil Rights. But the emotional emptiness in his marriage had reached a point in which he realized that he could no longer pretend. "I left my wife and child," he admits. "It was the worst thing I've done in my life."

In 1982, Clarence was named chairman of the Equal Employment Opportunity Commission (EEOC). During this time, he tried to reconcile with his wife, but they ended up separating again — this time for good. In 1983, his grandparents died within a month of each other, leaving him grief stricken. In 1984, his divorce was finalized, and his son, Jamal, came to live with him.

It was this series of painful crises in his personal life that carried Clarence Thomas back to God. "I was so unhappy that I started going to church again," he recalls. "St. Joseph's on Capitol Hill was only a short walk from my new office, and I went there each weekday to ask God to give me the wisdom to know what was right and the courage to do it — though I still couldn't bring myself to go to Sunday Mass. I wasn't yet ready to take that leap of faith."

When Bad Things Happen

A crisis in someone's life — illness, the death of a loved one, divorce, a job loss, or some unexpected tragedy — can

> *trigger a desire to turn to God or to the Catholic Church.*
> *When bad things happen, people feel as if they have lost*
> *their bearings. They can no longer rely on themselves, and*
> *they begin to search for something that they can hold on*
> *to for strength and for comfort. If you are going through*
> *a difficult time, but you're not ready to talk to a priest, try*
> *going to Mass. Or simply go into a Catholic church and sit*
> *before the Blessed Sacrament. Ask the Lord to give you the*
> *strength and the comfort that you need.*

In the spring of 1986, Clarence Thomas met Virginia Lamp, a labor-relations lobbyist for the U.S. Chamber of Commerce. Their friendship blossomed, and in 1987 they were married in a Methodist church. Together, they joined an Episcopal church, which they attended every Sunday — but during the week, Clarence still went to Mass.

Two years later, President George H. W. Bush appointed Clarence Thomas to the U.S. Court of Appeals in the District of Columbia Circuit. When Supreme Court Justice Thurgood Marshall announced his decision to retire, President Bush nominated Clarence Thomas as a replacement. The confirmation process was difficult, with horrible accusations against him.

"It had long since become clear to me that this battle was at bottom spiritual, not political," he explains, "and so my attention shifted from politics to the inward reality of my spiritual life."

He described it as a dark night of the soul. He knew that his enemies wanted to break his spirit so that he would walk away, but he felt that he owed it to his family and to the memory of his grandparents to confront the truth. During his appearances before the Senate Judiciary Committee, he denied every allegation that had been leveled against him. He later revealed that throughout the ordeal he found strength in God. After a Senate vote on October 15, 1991, the president's nominee was confirmed. Eight days later, when Clarence Thomas was sworn in as the 106th associate justice of the Supreme Court, President Bush commented: "America is blessed to have a man of this character serve on its highest court."

Clarence Thomas acknowledges the dark days during the confirmation hearings but notes that on this sunny day, there was joy. "I was alluding to Psalm 30, which had brought me much comfort in recent weeks and from which a friend had suggested that I quote on this great day: 'I will praise you, LORD, for you have rescued me. You refused to let my enemies triumph over me.... Weeping may go on all night, but joy comes with the morning.' I had forgotten that it was possible to know such joy. Thanks to God's direct intervention, I had risen phoenix-like from the ashes of self-pity and despair, and though my wounds were still raw, I trusted that in time they, too, would heal."

During this time, Clarence Thomas continued to attend morning Mass but officially remained a member of the Episcopal Church. The turning point came when he finally admitted to himself and to his wife that he wanted to return to the Catholic Church.

On June 8, 1996, Clarence Thomas announced to classmates at a Holy Cross reunion banquet that he had officially returned to the Catholic Church. He had received Communion that morning for the first time in 28 years. He had been granted a decree of nullity from his first marriage, and his marriage to Virginia had been convalidated. He had forgiven the Catholic Church for the racism he experienced in the seminary.

"Years later, I would find out, as you get older, that it is not the religion that is the problem," he admits. "It is the fallibility and imperfection of man."

When Someone Is Hurt by the Church

Hurts happen because the Catholic Church is made up of human beings. We may hold the Church to a higher ideal, but the reality is that people in the Church make mistakes. This has been true throughout the history of Christianity.

Jesus struggled with His apostles, who misunderstood Him, denied Him, betrayed Him, fell asleep when He asked them to pray, and ran away when He was arrested. Arguments arose among early Christians over religious beliefs and practices. Many saints suffered because of someone or something in the Church. The fact that the Church has survived 2,000 years in spite of human weakness is an indication that the Holy Spirit has kept the Catholic Church alive and growing.

If you've been hurt by someone or something in the Church, it's a good idea to talk about your experience with a priest, deacon, or pastoral associate. Try to separate your anger toward the person in the Church who hurt you and the Church itself. It wasn't the Church that caused the pain; rather, the pain was caused by a human being who was connected to the Church in one way or another. Pray for the wisdom to see the difference, and ask the Lord to shower you with His healing love.

For Additional Information

- Clarence Thomas, *My Grandfather's Son: A Memoir* (HarperCollins, 2007).
- Kevin Merida and Michael A. Fletcher, *Supreme Discomfort: The Divided Soul of Clarence Thomas* (Doubleday, 2007).
- Ken Foskett, *Judging Thomas: The Life and Times of Clarence Thomas* (HarperCollins, 2004).
- Andrew Peyton Thomas, *Clarence Thomas: A Biography* (Encounter Books, 2001).
- U.S. Bishops, "Discrimination and Christian Conscience," from *Pastoral Letters of the American Hierarchy, 1792-1970* (Our Sunday Visitor, 1971).
- U.S. Bishops, "Brothers and Sisters to Us: U.S. Catholic Bishops' Pastoral Letter on Racism in Our Day" (USCCB, 1979).

Amy Betros

Amy Betros is the cofounder of St. Luke's Mission of Mercy, which serves the battered, the broken, and the poorest of the poor in Buffalo, New York. She underwent a dramatic conversion and came back to the Church in 1989.

AMY BETROS was born into a faith-filled Maronite Catholic family in Buffalo, New York, on April 11, 1954. "My mother was from Lebanon, and my dad was a first-generation Lebanese American," she explains. "One of my earliest memories is that people from Lebanon would live with us while my parents helped them get settled in their own homes."

Amy's mother cooked large meals every day because they never knew how many people would come for dinner. After Mass on Sundays, Amy's father would invite to their home widows, widowers, and anyone else who didn't have a place to go. "I didn't know at the time that my parents were doing 'works of mercy,' " Amy recalls. "I just knew that it helped people, and it was what God wanted us to do."

Amy's parents eventually opened a bakery. At age 8, Amy didn't like having to help out, but she and her father came up with the idea that if they made it fun by singing and playing games, it wouldn't really be work. It's a philosophy that she has continued to practice in her life.

By the time Amy reached high school, she wanted to become a nun. The Franciscan sisters advised her to get a college degree and work for a while before entering their community. Deeply disappointed, Amy followed their advice and began taking courses at a Catholic college. She hated school and tried another Catholic college but ended up leaving for a job in the collections department at a bank.

It was a difficult time for Amy. She had always had a strong relationship with God, but she found herself upset with God because her life was not turning out the way she had expected. Her anger at the Franciscans also increased, and she began to feel that they had rejected her.

Before long, her anger spilled over into other areas of her spiritual life. When her local parish cancelled a Mass in order to have an antiwar demonstration, she was outraged and stopped going to Sunday Mass. At first, she still made visits to the Blessed Sacrament to talk with Jesus about what was going on in her life, but eventually, even that stopped.

How Faith Develops

Turning away from religion as a teenager or young adult often plays an important role in a person's faith journey.

There are several different theories about faith development. Most identify four distinct stages:

- **Childhood faith:** *Young children accept the religious beliefs and practices that their parents pass on to them. During this stage of faith development, children identify faith as something that is part of family life. It has no personal implications for them.*
- **Belonging faith:** *As children get older, they develop a sense of belonging to a parish. They attend religious-education classes, participate in liturgies, join in service projects, and get involved in youth events and activities. During this time, they begin to identify themselves as being Catholic, and they begin to understand that there are moral guidelines and responsibilities involved with being part of the Church.*
- **Questioning faith:** *During adolescence and young adulthood, questions and doubts arise. This is a transition stage when young people have to let go of their childhood faith so that they can grow into an adult faith relationship with God and the Catholic Church. This is a difficult time when young people feel alone, confused, and sometimes angry. During this stage, they either continue their search for God or they remain stuck in this transition and continue to struggle throughout their lives with unresolved questions, doubts, anger, and resentment.*
- **Committed faith:** *The culmination of the faith journey leads people to the point where they develop their own personal relationship with God and make an adult faith commitment. As the soon-to-be Pope*

> Benedict XVI explained: "An 'adult' faith is not a faith that follows the trends of fashion and the latest novelty; a mature adult faith is deeply rooted in friendship with Christ. It is this friendship that opens us up to all that is good and gives us a criterion by which to distinguish the true from the false, and deception from truth. We must develop this adult faith; we must guide the flock of Christ to this faith. And it is this faith — only faith — that creates unity and is fulfilled in love" (April 18, 2005).

In 1981, with her parents' help, Amy left her job at the bank and opened her own restaurant. She called it "Amy's Place," and the little storefront was open for breakfast, lunch, and dinner.

"I worked seven days a week," Amy recalls, "and the restaurant turned out to be more than a place where people could eat. It offered me the opportunity to help people in the same way my parents had helped people. When people needed food, financial help, or advice, they would come. The restaurant was always busy. I wasn't making a fortune, but I was making a difference in people's lives."

In 1989, Amy's cousin went on a pilgrimage to Medjugorje, where the Blessed Virgin Mary was reportedly appearing to a group of young people. Amy had never heard about it before, but when her cousin returned, Amy could see that she had been deeply moved.

"When I asked her what Our Lady was saying through the messages, she told me: 'God is upset with His people because they have left the churches. God wants everyone to return to Him.'"

The words struck at the core of Amy's heart. "I realized that I was one of those people upsetting God!" she admits.

Marian Apparitions in Medjugorje

In March 2010, an international commission of inquiry was appointed by the Vatican to investigate the reported apparitions of Our Lady in Medjugorje. The apparitions began in 1981 when six young people said that Our Lady had appeared to them. Since then, more than 30 million people have visited the small Bosnian town.

During the investigation, the commission will study the content of the messages received and whether the messages are in keeping with Catholic beliefs. They will also study the lives of the visionaries to make sure there is no deception or delusion. The commission will report their findings to the Congregation for the Doctrine of the Faith.

On Christmas that year, Amy experienced what she calls "a St. Paul conversion." Her uncle from Lebanon had come to visit, and he was "reading" the coffee grounds in Amy's cup. "The Blessed Mother loves you very much," he told her. "Your life will change, but you must go to the church closest to you. She is waiting for you there."

Overwhelmed, Amy decided to think about it for a while. When she got home, she discovered a newspaper that someone had left for her. The headline read, "Our Lady Queen of Peace Visits Medjugorje." Amy began to weep, and the tears continued for seven days. "People thought I was having a nervous breakdown," she recalls.

On New Year's Eve, Amy was working in the restaurant when a television documentary about Medjugorje came on the screen. The film chronicled the visit of Hollywood actor Martin Sheen to Medjugorje with a group of American pilgrims. It included interviews with some of the visionaries and comments by Church officials. It also showed the impact that the pilgrimage had on some of the Americans and some of the spiritual insights that they had experienced.

"For one solid hour, the whole restaurant seemed to stop," Amy recalls. "I cried through the entire program."

When the program ended, Amy went to the Catholic church across the street, knelt before the statue of the Blessed Mother, and consecrated her life to Our Lady. In her mind's eye, Amy saw herself as a little girl, watching the movie *The Song of Bernadette* and telling the Blessed Mother: *If only you would appear while I am alive, I would give you my life.* Amy felt as if her childhood promise was now being fulfilled.

Amy's life changed radically from that moment. She went to confession for the first time in 18 years and felt as if a "200-pound boulder" had been lifted from her. "Later, one of my customers commented that I was glowing," she recalls. "God had just given me the grace to recognize sins I had committed for 18 years, and then He forgave them in an instant!"

In May 1990, Amy went to Medjugorje and formally consecrated her life to Jesus through Our Lady. Over the course of the next two years, the Holy Spirit began to prepare Amy for the work that He wanted her to do. "He used my restaurant as a training ground and taught me not to be afraid," she explains.

Strangers began to tell her that as they passed the restaurant, they would hear a strange interior voice telling them: "Go inside. She will feed you." Often, it wasn't edible food that they were seeking but spiritual food. Amy would pray with people. She gave away medals, holy cards, and rosaries. It wasn't just Catholics who came. Muslims, Jews, atheists, young people, old people, the wealthy, and the poor found their way to Amy.

"God showed me how to love them all with truth and kindness," she explains. "To me, they were all children of God."

During this time, Amy formed a prayer group that helped to sustain her in what she now considered her restaurant ministry. She stockpiled clothing, canned goods, and toys for distribution to poor families. She took homeless prostitutes and drug addicts into her home — and even after they stole from her, Amy was not discouraged. She went out to parishes and community groups to show the Medjugorje documentary and tell the story of her decision to come back to the Catholic Church. She felt as if she had been called to witness to the way God had changed her life.

But even in the midst of all this activity, there was something missing. She felt as if the Holy Spirit was trying to lead her in a new direction. She just wasn't clear where she was being led.

God's plan for Amy began to unfold in 1992, when Auxiliary Bishop Edward M. Grosz of Buffalo invited her to accompany him on a pilgrimage to Fátima. The trip was another turning point. "When I went to Medjugorje, I discovered that Jesus loved me," she recalls. "In Fátima, I fell in love with Jesus in a spiritually deep and mature way. I felt a true freedom from worldly things, and all I cared about was doing His will," she recalls.

It was during this trip to Fátima that Amy met Norm Paolini, a researcher at a local cancer hospital, who shared Amy's devotion to the Blessed Mother and her passion for works of mercy. A short time later, Amy and Norm learned that the diocese was selling the property at St. Luke's Parish in the inner city, which had been closed as part of diocesan downsizing. Amy began to sense that the Blessed Mother wanted them to buy it.

She told Bishop Grosz that she and Norm would use the property to start an independent Catholic mission that would not rely on government subsidies or diocesan funding. The mission would run totally on trust in God. The bishop felt certain that this was God's will. So Amy sold her restaurant, Norm took an early retirement, and with the help of a generous benefactor they bought the parish buildings, which included a church, rectory, convent, and school.

On August 1, 1994, they opened St. Luke's Mission of Mercy in one of the poorest, most crime-ridden and drug-infested neighborhoods in Buffalo. "We promised the Lord that we would accept the most abandoned, and He has tested us to the hilt!" Amy admits.

Today, St. Luke's serves meals to an average of 400 people daily. It offers shelter to men and women of all ages. Families receive emergency housing in neighborhood homes that have been donated to the mission and restored by volunteers. The first floor of the school building has been transformed into "St. Luke's Mall," with clothing, small appliances, and household goods that have been donated by generous and loving people.

Amy is careful, however, to distinguish between the ministry of St. Luke's and the role of a social worker: "We ask people, 'What do you need? How can we help you?' But our primary goal is to bring people to the Lord. That means we have to live the Gospel ourselves."

The Desire to Help Others

People who feel drawn back to the Catholic Church are often motivated by a desire to help others. There are many opportunities in the secular world to help other people. What's missing is the spiritual dimension that service within a Catholic framework provides. It stems from our belief that we are all part of the Mystical Body of Christ and that when one part of the Body is hurting, hungry, or in distress, we all suffer.

Amy's efforts to follow in Christ's footsteps have attracted hundreds of people who want to help as volunteers, benefactors, and friends. Fifteen of them have given up their jobs to live at St. Luke's as "missionaries." St. Luke's also has its own Jesuit chaplain, Father Jack Mattimore.

With each passing year, new ministries emerge. There is Good Shepherd Residence, for men recovering from drug and alcohol addictions, and Our Lady of Hope Home School, which offers Catholic education to students from prekindergarten through the eighth grade. St. Luke's missionaries visit the sick, comfort people who are in difficult situations, and offer Catholic funerals and burials for anyone in need. The Voices of Mercy, a vocal and instrumental group, provides music for liturgies, retreats, and local concerts. Amy and Norm also have their own weekly radio show, *Mercy Times*.

"Since the beginning, we have included Jesus in the Eucharist and the guidance of a priest in every decision and every stage of development," Amy says. "This has been the key to the mission's success. We are committed to God's call to evangelize, to preach the Good News of Jesus Christ with our lives, and to bring the love and mercy of God to those who feel abandoned by Him."

Amy believes that the greatest tragedy in today's society is that people don't understand what it means to be loved by God.

"People come to St. Luke's every day for one reason or another — food or a bed, help with a utility bill, or help dealing with a social-services nightmare — but those aren't the real reasons," she explains. "People come here because they don't feel loved. I'd have to be dead or a fool to not see God working in the lives of these people. The most beautiful thing I've seen is people who didn't even have a family before, and now the Lord is showing them what family is and what love really is. Everything that happens here is just another sign of God's merciful love."

For Additional Information

- Elizabeth Ficocelli, *The Fruits of Medjugorje: Stories of True and Lasting Conversion* (Paulist Press, 2006).

- *Medjugorje: The Lasting Sign (An Extensive and Thought-Provoking Documentary of the Apparitions of the Blessed Virgin Mary in Medjugorje)*, hosted and narrated by Martin Sheen, produced by Rob Wallace (Medjugorje Partners, Inc., 1988).

Website

- St. Luke's Mission of Mercy: *www.stlukesmissionofmercy.org*

Martin Sheen

Martin Sheen, an award-winning actor, has appeared in
over 140 motion pictures and television programs.
He reclaimed his Catholic faith in 1981.

MARTIN SHEEN was born into a devout Catholic family on
August 3, 1940, in Dayton, Ohio. His father came from
Spain and his mother from Ireland. He was the first of his 10
siblings to be born in the United States, and he was baptized
Ramón Antonio Gerard Estévez.

"I grew up in a very traditional Catholic-immigrant
family," he recalls. He attended Catholic grammar school,
served as an altar boy, and graduated from an all-boys Catholic high school.

He also developed a strong sense of social justice. As a
young teenager, Ramón organized a strike of golf caddies at
the local country club in protest of the abusive language and
racist, anti-Semitic comments made by the club members.

When his father disapproved of his plans to become an actor, 18-year-old Ramón purposely failed the entrance exam for the University of Dayton, borrowed money for bus fare from a Catholic priest, and went to New York City to pursue his dream. He adopted the stage name "Martin," after a close friend, and "Sheen," after Archbishop Fulton J. Sheen. But he never legally changed his name.

While he was learning the art of acting, he became involved with the Living Theater, an alternative theater on 14th Street that staged poetic dramas and unconventional plays. Through Julian Beck, a director at the Living Theater, Martin Sheen discovered Dorothy Day and the Catholic Worker movement. At first, he started going to the Catholic Worker House in lower Manhattan because he was a struggling actor, and they would give him a free meal. But he soon began to admire their work and started to volunteer.

The Catholic Worker

The Catholic Worker movement was started in 1933, during the depths of the Great Depression, by Dorothy Day, a journalist who converted to Catholicism, and Peter Maurin, a French immigrant who was committed to Catholic social justice. They began their ministry by publishing a newspaper called the Catholic Worker, *which explained Catholic social teaching. It wasn't long before they opened what they called a "House of Hospitality" to serve the needs of the poor and the homeless in the slums of New York City.*

Peter Maurin died in 1949, but Dorothy Day continued to write and speak about Catholic social issues until her death in 1980. Her cause for canonization is currently being investigated by the Catholic Church.

In 1996, the movie Entertaining Angels: The Story of Dorothy Day *was released. Moira Kelly played Dorothy Day, and Martin Sheen played Peter Maurin.*

Today, the nearly 200 Catholic Worker communities in the United States and throughout the world remain committed to the principles of nonviolence, voluntary poverty, prayer, and hospitality to those in need.

In December 1961, Martin Sheen married Janet Templeton. In 1964, he landed his first major role in the Broadway play *The Subject Was Roses.* During this time, when he was busy building his acting career and starting a family, he began to drift away from the practice of his Catholic faith. He was never opposed to Catholicism, but as his career became more demanding with roles in major motion pictures and television movies, he stopped going to Mass. "I lived for many years without faith," he admits.

Everything changed in 1977, when Martin suffered a heart attack. It happened while he was in the Philippines working on the movie *Apocalypse Now.* He received the anointing of the sick, and he recovered physically. Fear of death brought him back to the Church, but his new devotion gradually faded as he began to drink more heavily. "I was divided inside: I had no spirituality," he recalls.

In 1981, Martin took a small part in the movie *Gandhi,* and while he was in India for the filming, he was overwhelmed by the poverty and the human degradation. Afterward, he spent three months in Paris working on another film. It gave him time to reflect on his life and what he had experienced in India. He was staying across the street from St. Joseph Church, and he began to attend the English-language Mass.

During this period, he also reconnected with an old friend, Terry Malick, who had directed him in the movie *Badlands*. Malick recognized that Martin was on a spiritual quest and started giving him books to read. The last book he gave him was Fyodor Dostoevsky's *The Brothers Karamazov*. Martin was moved by the dramatic interplay of faith, doubt, moral struggle, passion, pain, and free will in the book. He suddenly felt as if God was calling him to come back to the Church.

On May 1, 1981, he read the final chapter of *The Brothers Karamazov*, put down the book, and walked over to St. Joseph's Church. The door was locked because it was a national holiday. He went to the rectory and rang the bell. When no one answered, he started pounding on the door. Just as he began to think that maybe this was not what God wanted him to do, a priest opened the door.

"I'm sorry to bother you, Father, but I've been away from the Church many years, and I'd like to come back," Martin said. "I'd like to go to confession."

He knew by the way the priest looked at him that he had done the right thing. After pouring out all of his pain and his brokenness, the priest gave him absolution and said, "Welcome back."

In that encounter with God's grace, Martin Sheen's fear of dying was replaced with intense joy and the desire to live the remainder of his life to the fullest. For the first time, he felt truly free.

How to Go to Confession

Many people who have been away from the Church for a long time worry about what to say and do in confession.

You can start with the words from a prayer that you probably learned as a child: "Bless me, Father, for I have sinned. It has been a long time since my last confession." Or you can simply say to the priest, "I've been away from the Church for a long time, and I was hoping you could help me make a good confession."

Most priests realize how uncomfortable you feel and will try to put you at ease. The priest might ask what kept you away for so long or what prompted you to come back. No priest will expect you to remember every sin that you committed since your last confession. Some will lead you through the Ten Commandments as a way of making a general confession. Others will ask you if there is a particular sin you've been carrying all these years that you want to mention.

The priest might also help you to recall little sins, which can pile up over the years. He might pose questions such as these: "Do you sometimes think of yourself before thinking of others? Do you overindulge in any way? Do you take good care of yourself? Do you pray? Do you carry any prejudices in your heart? Do you use your gifts and talents wisely? Do you sometimes talk about people behind their backs? Do you ever twist the truth? Have you ever cheated? Are you struggling to forgive someone? Do you have questions or concerns about your relationship with God?"

When you have finished, the priest will ask you to express sorrow for your sins. If you don't remember the Act of Contrition, you can tell God that you are sorry in your own words, or you can ask the priest to help you. You will be given some kind of penance — often prayers or some act of charity. Then the priest will give you absolution, bless you, and welcome you back.

Martin Sheen's return to the Church stirred in him a passion for nonviolence and social justice that he had first experienced as a boy. "We have to find God's presence, first of all, in our own brokenness," he explains. "Then we have to find it in service. We grow by serving."

Today, Martin considers himself a "radical" Catholic. In the early 1980s, he actively protested the political atrocities in Central America, took a stand against American aid to the government of El Salvador, and worked toward better political-asylum policies in the United States. His first civil-disobedience arrest was in 1986 while protesting President Ronald Reagan's "Star Wars" initiative.

Over the past 30 years, Martin has been arrested more than 60 times for civil disobedience. He admits that he doesn't know if civil disobedience has any effect on government-policy changes but adds that "it has a great effect on the person who chooses to do it."

Martin acknowledges that his involvement in peace and social justice stems from his faith and his conscience. He feels as if he has been led by the Holy Spirit to just be a presence to the marginal and a voice for the voiceless. "And sometimes, it's very costly," he admits. "But it's also very freeing, because in every one of the arrests I've been involved in, I have been satisfied in my conscience that I did everything I possibly could, and I did it nonviolently, and I tried to do it humanely and even joyfully. So that's the major criteria I use for involvement."

He supports Consistent Life, a group committed to the protection of life. And he has publicly stated that while he would never "judge" a woman who aborted a child, he is opposed to abortion because "as a father and a grandfather, I have had experience with children who don't always come when they are planned, and I have experienced the great joy of God's presence in my children. But I am equally against the death penalty or war — anywhere people are sacrificed for some end justifying a means."

He took part in the 2006-2007 immigration marches in Los Angeles. He appeared in radio and television ads urging voters in Washington State to oppose assisted suicide. He is an advocate for fair wages and serves as spokesman for the United Farm Workers. He opposes war but supports the soldiers as human beings. He has personally delivered food to poor families in Los Angeles at Thanksgiving time and volunteered in a soup kitchen that serves the homeless.

What Is a Consistent Life Ethic?

In 1983, Cardinal Joseph Bernardin (1928-1996) introduced the concept of a consistent life ethic to promote the idea that abortion, assisted suicide, euthanasia, capital punishment, unjust war, nuclear war, genetic engineering, hunger, poverty, and economic injustice are all respect-life issues.

"When human life is considered 'cheap' or easily expendable in one area, eventually nothing is held as sacred, and all lives are in jeopardy," Cardinal Bernardin explained.

In his 1995 encyclical The Gospel of Life, *Pope John Paul II pointed out that the right to life is the foundation for all other human rights. He explained: "The deepest element of God's commandment to protect human life is the requirement to show reverence and love for every person and the life of every person" (n. 41).*

> *The concept of respecting life is so profound that it's worth meditating upon. When people embrace the concept of respecting life, that concept affects everything they say and do.*

Today, Martin Sheen carries a rosary in his pocket, which he says keeps him from cursing. He attends Mass faithfully and is an active member of his parish. "As the Mass begins and the crucifix in the central nave comes close, I think: *I know this man. He is my redeemer. He also belongs to me.*"

From 1999 until 2006, he played the role of Josiah Bartlet, the fictional president of the United States on the television series *The West Wing*. His character just happened to be Catholic, and the show included scenes where he was praying the Rosary, seeking guidance from a priest, and using a coffee mug from the University of Dayton, the Catholic college that Martin Sheen's father wanted him to attend so many years earlier.

"I have not always practiced my Catholicism," Martin admits. "I left it as a youth, and I lived for many years without faith.... When I returned to the Church, I had been away for 15 years, perhaps more. I had no love, no respect. So for me, the moment I was born to the faith... I knew it.... I thought: *I am home. I am home. I am free.*"

He offers the following advice to people who are feeling drawn back to the Catholic Church:

It's about faith. The fact that you feel drawn back to church is the grace. Don't worry about anything.

Just follow God's grace. We are all entitled to God's grace. Grace is a gift, and you shouldn't be afraid to claim it. Coming back to the Church is a choice that you make. I made that choice. I go to Mass because I choose to — not because I have to. It takes a lot of courage to accept responsibility for our faith. It is faith that brings me to the sacraments, and no one can take that away from me.

For Additional Information

- Lee Riley and David Shumacher, *The Sheens: Martin, Charlie, and Emilio Estevez* (St. Martin's Press, 1989).
- "Martin Sheen Interview," David Kupfer, *The Progressive* (July 2003).
- "Martin Sheen: Catholic President on Prime Time," Greg Heffernan, *St. Anthony Messenger* (May 2000).

Websites

- Martin Sheen biography: *www.filmreference.com/film/28/Martin-Sheen*
- The Catholic Worker movement: *www.catholicworker.org*
- Consistent Life: *www.consistent-life.org*

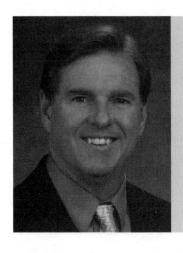

Dr. Kevin Vost

Kevin Vost, Psy.D., is a clinical psychologist who taught psychology at the University of Illinois at Springfield, Lincoln Land Community College, and MacMurray College. He served on the Research Review Committee for American Mensa. A former power lifter and weight-lifting instructor, he lives in Springfield, Illinois, with his wife and two sons. He travels extensively, giving talks about his books and his return to the Catholic Church.

KEVIN VOST has fond memories of growing up Catholic in Springfield, Illinois. His mother was an Irish Catholic. His father was a convert from Methodism. Kevin and his siblings were enrolled in St. Agnes Catholic School, where the Dominican sisters formed them in the Catholic faith, with reverence for Christ and the Church, a firm sense of right and wrong, and the conviction that we are called to treat one another with love.

The Vost family went to Mass every Sunday, but there were no outward signs of Catholic devotion in their household. "Our family didn't really talk about faith at home," Kevin recalls. "We did not pray together, and when I had to have a Bible for high school religion class, my mom had to take me to the Marian Center to buy one." Looking back, he described himself as "a Catholic-educated, Mass-going, altar-serving, nominal Catholic."

During high school, several friends started attending a Bible-based Pentecostal church. Kevin tagged along and came to the conclusion that if everything he had learned about Jesus was true, he should try to follow in the footsteps of Christ. He read Christian books, watched evangelists on television, and enjoyed sharing spiritual insights with his "born-again" friends, but he never felt any desire to leave the Catholic faith. In fact, during his freshman year in college, he talked with a seminarian about the possibility of becoming a priest.

Everything changed, however, when he began reading atheistic philosophers such as Friedrich Nietzsche, Bertrand Russell, and Ayn Rand. By age 20, Kevin came to believe that "existence exists." He saw God as superfluous, unnecessary, self-contradictory, and unreal. "It was not that I openly rejected God or the moral teachings of the Church," he explains. "I had simply been led to think that while I would have liked for God to exist, I could not in good conscience believe it!"

Twenty-three years passed before Kevin Vost changed his mind. In the meantime, he earned a master's degree and a doctorate in psychology. He married his wife, Kathy, in 1984, and they had two sons: Eric in 1986 and Kyle in 1992.

Because Kevin valued the intellectual and moral training he had received as a child, the decision was made to send the children to Catholic schools. "I even went to Mass at times," he recalls. "I basically believed that the Catholic Church possessed many wonderful things — but God was not one of them!"

His rediscovery of faith was more of a process than an event. It started in 2003 when he began listening to a series of audio lectures on Greek and Roman Stoic philosophers. He enjoyed the series so much that he ordered a lecture on Aristotle that was taught by Father Joseph Koterski, a Catholic priest. Father Koterski piqued Kevin's interest, and Kevin ordered another lecture on natural law, which introduced him to St. Thomas Aquinas.

St. Thomas Aquinas

St. Thomas Aquinas (1225-1274), a Dominican priest born in Aquino, Italy, is considered to be the greatest theologian and philosopher in the Catholic Church. His writings on natural law, ethics, virtues, the nature of God, and political theory are so fundamental that a great deal of modern philosophy is a reaction in favor of or against his writings.

His best-known work is his Summa Theologica. *It includes five arguments for the existence of God. It also explores creation, the human being, Jesus Christ, the sacraments, and the purpose of life. St. Thomas had not completed this work at the time of his death. Before he died, he had an overwhelming mystical experience of God that led him to declare that everything he had written seemed like straw when compared to the reality of God.*

Kevin began to see the Stoics, Aristotle, and St. Thomas Aquinas as interlocking keys to an authentic understanding of humanity. The Stoics understood how to control emotions through the proper use of reason. Aristotle understood how the human mind functions and established a system of logic. Both the Stoics and Aristotle glorified the pursuit of virtue to achieve perfection and happiness.

In the writings of St. Thomas Aquinas, however, Kevin saw the ancient philosophers in a Christian context. The fact that these philosophers all believed in God intrigued him. For the first time, he began to see the inadequacies of the atheistic philosophers that he had followed earlier in his life. Their arguments were not as airtight as he had originally thought. He remembers wondering if he had been "intellectually presumptuous" in insisting that there was no God.

"It was my firsthand immersion in the writings of St. Thomas Aquinas that brought me to the intellectual 'aha' experience that removed my blinders to the compatibility of faith and reason, and most important, to the reality of God," Kevin admits. "I did not know until I was back in the Church that Leo XIII had said in *Aeterni Patris* in 1879 that modern scientific-minded people would be most likely to return to the Church through the writings of the great Scholastic philosophers and theologians such as St. Thomas Aquinas. Well, 125 years after Pope Leo wrote that, it happened to me!"

St. Thomas Aquinas led Kevin to St. Augustine, St. Clement of Alexandria, and other Fathers of the Church. He developed a profound appreciation for the depth and beauty of sacred Scripture. He experienced the reality of God, and it brought him back into full communion with the Catholic Church.

Who Are the Church Fathers?

The Church Fathers were theologians, teachers, bishops, and popes, primarily from the first eight centuries of the Christian era, whose teachings laid the foundation for Catholic doctrine. They include Clement of Rome, Ignatius of Antioch, Polycarp of Smyrna, Clement of Alexandria, Athanasius of Alexandria, John Chrysostom, Cyril of Alexandria, Basil of Caesarea, Gregory Nazianzen, Peter of Sebaste, Gregory of Nyssa, Maximus the Confessor, Tertullian, Cyprian of Carthage, Ambrose of Milan, Jerome, Augustine of Hippo, Gregory the Great, and John Damascene, who is usually considered to be the last of the Church Fathers.

Also influential in early Christian theology were the Desert Fathers, who lived as hermits in the Egyptian desert. Their ideas are collected in Apophthegmata Patrum *("Sayings of the Fathers").*

Kevin remembers feeling relieved, contented, and at peace. "Now I could be a part of my Church community without feeling like an outsider on the inside," he explains. "I could join in on a 2,000-year-old tradition incredibly rich in history, theology, philosophy, art, architecture, music, spiritual truths, and charitable works. I could begin a journey of growing in knowledge of the faith and in learning how to live it. I now think about God every day. I try to think, feel, and act in accordance with the laws He has established to bring us true happiness in this life and the next."

But Kevin's return to the faith was not without complications. Over the years, he had cultivated a reputation as an intellectual, and some of his friends and co-workers questioned his changing attitudes and behaviors. "The popular media in this country has strongly, and to a large extent successfully, promoted the idea that brains and religion don't mix," he explains. "We are led to believe that to embrace belief in God, you have to shut down parts of your intellect and throw science and reason out the window. This is utter nonsense. When I came back to the Church, I threw none of my old knowledge out the window. I simply recognized that much of what I used to see as complete truths were merely partial truths."

Kevin also became somewhat apprehensive about the attitudes and behaviors of friends and associates who were not grounded in faith. "I found myself trying to figure out how to walk the fine line by remaining a friend or colleague without endorsing certain behaviors. In a nutshell, I tried to back off on the activities that could lead to problems without rejecting those friends, and I tried to cultivate new friendships with people who were more focused on the things of God."

Perhaps the greatest surprise was the opportunity to put his knowledge and experience to good use within the context of the Catholic faith. It started with the realization that St. Thomas Aquinas and St. Albert the Great were instrumental in developing memory strategies in the 13th century. Kevin had done his master's thesis on memory training and techniques, but his new focus on faith helped him see it from a different perspective. He contacted a Catholic publisher and ended up writing *Memorize the Faith! (And Most Anything Else) Using the Methods of the Great Catholic Medieval Memory Masters.*

St. Albert the Great

St. Albert the Great was born in Germany at the turn of the 13th century. Recognized as "the teacher of everything there is to know," St. Albert was a Dominican priest, natural scientist, philosopher, theologian, bishop, and adviser to the pope. He was both a teacher and a mentor to St. Thomas Aquinas. He believed that all of creation reflected God's wisdom and power. He died in Cologne in 1280.

Kevin also parlayed his past experience in strength and endurance training into the book *Fit for Eternal Life: A Christian Approach to Working Out, Eating Right, and Building the Virtues of Fitness in Your Soul.*

Kevin's next project focused on what he had learned about virtues from St. Thomas Aquinas. He transformed it into *Unearthing Your Ten Talents: A Thomistic Guide to Spiritual Growth.* He tells his own story of conversion and coming back to the Church in *From Atheism to Catholicism: How Scientists and Philosophers Led Me to Truth.* His newest book focuses on the life and lessons of St. Albert the Great.

"So in a sense, my major transition has been to follow the Holy Spirit's guidance in showing me how to turn what I learned in my decades without God into works for His greater glory," he says.

This transformation of Kevin's old life into a new life in Christ is also evident in his surroundings. His office contains a replica of a Roman centurion's helmet, a brass model of the Colosseum, a bust of Poseidon, an authentic Roman coin, a set of pens designed as Greek and Roman columns, a bust of Athena, and a Greek vase with scenes from the *Iliad.*

Recent additions to his collection include several crucifixes, a statue of St. Thomas Aquinas, and a portrait of the Virgin Mary holding Jesus and a baby lamb.

All of these objects are important to Kevin because Aristotle and St. Thomas Aquinas taught him the importance of using our senses. "Even our knowledge of God begins with things in the world we can see, hear, taste, and touch," he explains. "The things of the Church are absolutely beautiful. They are not something contrary or opposed to my Greek and Roman treasures. They are the completion and fruition."

Prayer, which was nonexistent in Kevin's life for 20 years, is now part of his daily routine. He incorporates spiritual reading; spontaneous prayer; formal prayers; calm, meditative prayers; and what he considers the best of all, attendance at Mass. He advises people who may feel drawn back to the Church to allow the Holy Spirit to guide them.

"If it is something that you feel in your heart, be aware that the Catholic Church holds an abundance of treasure for your mind as well," he explains. "There is no positive power in you that you will have to give up. The only thing you'll have to surrender is your will toward sin and your decision to separate yourself from God. Every day, seek to learn to love God with all your heart, mind, and soul. There is nothing more worthy of your efforts. Everything works according to God's plan as long as we work with Him."

For Additional Information

- Kevin Vost, *From Atheism to Catholicism: How Scientists and Philosophers Led Me to Truth* (Our Sunday Visitor, 2010).

- Kevin Vost, *A Great-Souled Man: The Life and Lessons of St. Albert the Great* (Tan Books, 2011).
- Kevin Vost, *Unearthing Your Ten Talents: A Thomistic Guide to Spiritual Growth* (Sophia Institute Press, 2010).
- Kevin Vost, *Fit for Eternal Life: A Christian Approach to Working Out, Eating Right, and Building the Virtues of Fitness in Your Soul* (Sophia Institute Press, 2007).
- Kevin Vost, *Memorize the Faith! (And Most Anything Else) Using the Methods of the Great Catholic Medieval Memory Masters* (Sophia Institute Press, 2006).

Websites:

- Kevin Vost: *www.drvost.com*
- *Aeterni Patris* (On the Restoration of Christian Philosophy), encyclical of Pope Leo XIII: *www.vatican.va/holy_father/leo_xiii /encyclicals/documents/hf_l-xiii_enc_04081879_aeterni-patris_en.html*

Leah Darrow

*Leah Darrow was a former contestant on the reality
show* America's Next Top Model *and worked as a
professional model in New York City before making a
decision to come back to the Catholic Church. She is now
a national Catholic speaker and a spokesperson for Pure
Fashion, an international ministry to teenage girls.
She lives in Eureka, Missouri.*

LEAH DARROW was born on June 24, 1979, in Norman,
Oklahoma. The oldest of six children, she grew up on a
farm, saying the Rosary with her family and attending Catholic schools. "My parents were amazing," she recalls. "Faith
was part of our daily conversation. They instilled in us a
love and trust of Christ Jesus."

It was their deep Catholic faith that sustained the family when an unthinkable tragedy struck. Leah was 12 years

old when her grandfather was murdered by one of the farm workers. After her parents received the call, they packed the children into the car and drove to St. James Church in Oklahoma City for 7 a.m. Mass. It made a profound impression on Leah. "I sat there in that church looking at Jesus on the cross and thinking: *The only one who knows my pain is God the Father because His Son was taken from Him.* Then it hit me: *This is where we go when things go bad.* We could barely hold ourselves up, but this is where we came. I knew that day that God would take care of us. I knew that I could trust God."

When Leah was a sophomore in high school, her father accepted a new job and moved the family to St. Louis, Missouri. During high school, Leah admits that her relationship with God and the Catholic Church became "a little fuzzy." By the time she was in college, she still thought of herself as a Catholic, but she was not really practicing her faith, and she really didn't agree with many of the teachings of the Church.

"I became the person who did whatever felt good, whatever was easiest, and whatever was the best for me," she admits. "I used to tell people that the Catholic Church was behind the times. It was an excuse. I was actually doing all of the things that the Church says not to do, so it was my way of justifying my own behavior."

She graduated with honors from the University of Missouri-St. Louis, where she earned a degree in psychology. She took a job as the assistant manager of a clothing store. She had just been offered a promotion when she was invited to interview for a reality series, *America's Next Top Model.*

It seemed like a great opportunity to Leah. While she was in college, she had done some modeling for local companies and had appeared in a few local television commercials.

She auditioned for the reality show in St. Louis and was selected as one of 40 semifinalists. The producers flew her to Los Angeles. The competition was intense, but Leah survived the next round of cuts and became one of 14 finalists, who were flown back to New York City for the final judging.

"It was overwhelming at times," she reveals. "Everything moved so fast that you didn't have time to think. You just did what they asked because you were afraid of being eliminated. They would put you in a beautiful room and tell you to wait there until they came for you. Sometimes they would come right away, and sometimes you would wait there for hours. You were also constantly aware of the camera recording everything you said and did. I always had the feeling that I was not good enough."

As part of the show, Leah endured some harsh criticism for not looking into the camera and not positioning herself well with the photographer during a photo shoot in Jamaica. But one of the cruelest remarks came from one of the judges, who asked Leah if she was a Catholic. When Leah replied that she was, the judge suggested that Leah read *The Da Vinci Code*, which presents the Catholic Church in an untrue and unfavorable way.

"I couldn't believe that she would say that to me," Leah recalls. "It was the first time my faith had been attacked in that way. But I didn't know what to say to her because I knew that I wasn't really living my faith."

Leah was eventually eliminated from the competition and went back to St. Louis, where she was greeted as a hometown celebrity. After all of the flattery and fame, she began to think that what she really wanted was to become a professional model. She decided to move back to New York

City, where she was offered contracts with several modeling agencies. Leah turned down the offers when she saw
how exploitive the contracts were, and she decided to try
to make it as an independent model. It wasn't long before
she began to get calls for modeling jobs. She was shocked at
how much money she started to make.

"We live in a culture of excess," Leah explains. "We
always want more...better...faster. We use people and
things. A lot of fashion models fall into bad situations, and I
was one of them. I was motivated by vanity and pride. I was
making bad decisions."

Leah was successful, but she was not really happy. "All
I wanted was to be loved," she admits. "I wanted attention."

Her last modeling job brought her to her knees. She had
been invited to do a photo shoot for a large international
magazine. They told her that she had not been on the reality show long enough to highlight all aspects of herself as
a model. They wanted to shoot the sultry, sexy side of her.
They assured her that this would be just what she needed to
boost her career.

Leah showed up for the photo shoot, had her hair and
makeup done, and then saw the wardrobe cart with very
skimpy outfits. She put one of them on and began posing for
the photographer. She felt uncomfortable in the outfit, but
she kept telling herself, "You're a professional. Just do it.
Just get it over with."

Leah could not sustain that train of thought, however.
"As more shots were being taken, I felt as if more and more
of me was being torn away," she explains. "I realized that in
grasping for all those hopes and dreams I had for this career,
I had fallen so far away from my true ideals."

In that moment, she had a mental image of herself in the same skimpy outfit standing before God at the moment of her death. Her hands were reaching out in a gesture of offering something to Him, but there was nothing in her hands. It occurred to her that all of her talents had been wasted. She had done nothing to help anyone but herself. She felt ashamed. Color drained from her face, and her skin turned pale. The photographer began saying, "Leah, are you all right?"

"I can't do this anymore," she replied. Then she ran out of the studio, got dressed, and left the building. She walked down Fifth Avenue sobbing. "I was so unhappy," she recalls. "All the things I thought I wanted, I had gotten, and I wasn't happy."

She went back to her apartment, and after more tears, the memory of sitting in church after her grandfather had died came back to her: *This is where we go when things go bad.* Leah realized that she had to leave New York. She had to go home. She called her father in St. Louis. "Dad, I want to come home," she sobbed. "If you don't come and get me, I'm going to lose my soul."

"Okay, baby," he replied. "I'm coming to get you."

When Childhood Memories Surface

The Lord sometimes draws us back to Himself through memories. Sometimes people recall childhood devotions to Our Lady or the saints. Memories of music, incense, a statue, or a crucifix from your parish church may surface. You might recall feeling the presence of God at your First Communion or confirmation. You might wonder if it

> *would ever be possible to recapture your childhood faith.*
> *You may wonder if you could ever feel completely con-*
> *nected to God again.*
>
> *The answer is yes. Think of yourself as being on a*
> *spiritual journey back in time. It's a good idea to record*
> *your memories in a spiritual journal. The more you write,*
> *the more memories will surface. When you're ready, talk*
> *to a priest about what you are experiencing. He can help*
> *you to discern where the Holy Spirit may be leading you.*

Leah admits that the time she spent waiting for her father to drive from St. Louis to New York City felt like a dark night of the soul. The story of her life kept replaying itself in her mind. She thought about all of the bad things she had done and all of the people she had hurt. She also worried about what her father would say to her when he arrived.

But her father greeted her with a huge smile and said, "I'm so happy to see you!" He told her that he wanted to see a little bit of New York before they left. He wanted to walk through Central Park and eat a Reuben sandwich at Carnegie Deli. Then he got very serious and said, "But first, you are going to confession!"

Leah was afraid to go to confession, and she suggested that it might be better to wait until they got back to St. Louis, but her father said no. "You said you wanted to come home," he told her. "You could have hopped on an airplane if you wanted to come back to Missouri, but you called me, and I'm taking you to church because the Catholic Church is the home that you need."

Looking back, Leah admits that it was nice to be pushed. "The weight of my sinfulness was so heavy that I felt as if I couldn't take a breath of fresh air," she explained.

They went to St. Rose of Lima Church in Brooklyn. There was a priest in the confessional, and when Leah knelt down she told him that she hadn't been to confession in a very long time. She admitted that she had a lot to say. But she really didn't want to say anything, because when you say something out loud, it becomes real, and she didn't want to admit some of the things she had done.

"Don't worry about what you're going to say," the priest told her. "I'm here to help, and we're going to get through this. Just tell me the absolute worst thing."

Leah told him, and then he asked her to tell him the next worst thing. "He led me right through it," she recalls. "He asked me if I ever did this or that. I would say yes or no. He basically went through the Ten Commandments. He told me what things were sins and what things weren't sins. He allowed me to organize my life — and once we had everything organized, he gave me absolution, and it all went away!"

Leah had heard people talk about feeling a sense of peace after going to confession, but she never understood what they meant until that moment. "I understood peace only in the context of war," she explained, "and there was finally no more war inside of me, only peace."

Overcoming a Fear of Confession

There are many reasons why people are afraid of confession. Some people have had bad experiences as a child. Some are afraid of going into a small, dark confessional.

Some recall harsh treatment by priests. Some might be so ashamed of something that they don't want to admit it to anyone. The problem with all of these things is that when we bury something negative, it stays inside of us, where it festers and causes us to feel unnecessary guilt, anger, and resentment. We sometimes have to expend a lot of energy to keep something below the surface. Confession gives us the chance to open old wounds and let the poison drain out. It is a healing process.

A few days later, Leah and her father drove back to St. Louis. It was difficult for her at first. She realized that she had to change some of the things in her life. "I stopped hanging out with certain people because they were doing things that I no longer wanted to do," she admits.

Before long, she met new friends and realized she could enjoy life in a completely different way. After a while, she started to volunteer with the youth group at her parish. She knew that God was calling her to do something worthwhile with her life. She was being called to use the talents God had given to her. She knew that in one way or another, she was being asked to help other people. What she didn't realize was that the Lord would use the two things that she had loved most — fashion and talking with people — as the basis for what would become her new life in Christ.

It was during this time that she learned about Pure Fashion, an international faith-based program for girls, ages 14 to 18, that includes training in fashion, runway modeling, personal presentation, and service. The goal is to help teens discover that their deepest beauty comes from being created in the image of God's love.

"I saw a story about it on EWTN," she recalls. "Here were these cute girls and adorable outfits being showcased on the Catholic channel. I checked out the Pure Fashion website and wrote them an e-mail thanking them for creating this ministry."

Brenda Sharman, national director of Pure Fashion, received the e-mail and called Leah on the telephone. They talked for a long time. Leah shared her modeling experiences and the story of her conversion. Brenda got Leah involved with Chicago's Pure Fashion team, and before long, Leah spearheaded the first Pure Fashion team in St. Louis. She also helped to start a chapter in Canada, and she has since been invited to visit a number of chapters around the country.

"Pure Fashion teaches girls about purity, modesty, and chastity in their words, actions, and dress," Leah explains. "There are many forces trying to tear at our dignity by telling us that we have to be something else. That is a lie. What we need is to try to live our lives according to the Gospel. In whatever way He calls us, we are strengthened by Christ. When we live for Christ, He gives us eternal life and love."

In addition to her work with Pure Fashion, Leah is also a speaker for Catholic Answers, a laity-run apologetics and evangelization ministry, and their sister company, Chastity.com. She speaks at conferences and in dioceses around the country with honesty, inspiration, and humor. By sharing her story, she hopes that people will see how Christ Jesus worked in her life — and through His love and mercy, brought her out of a very bad situation. It's not unusual for her to tell her audiences, "Ever hear that Prodigal Son story? I'm his sister!"

Websites

- Leah Darrow: *www.leahdarrow.com*
- Pure Fashion: *www.purefashion.com*
- Catholic Answers: *www.catholic.com*
- Chastity.com: *www.chastity.com*

Danny Abramowicz

*A former NFL player, he is now an author, speaker, and
television host of EWTN's* Crossing the Goal. *His
addiction to alcohol separated him from God and almost
destroyed his life. His recovery began in 1981.*

DANNY ABRAMOWICZ was born on July 13, 1945, into a
Catholic family in Steubenville, Ohio, a steel-mill and coal-
mining town near the West Virginia border. He attended
Mass with his parents, went to St. Peter's Catholic School,
and received a solid spiritual foundation as a young boy.

Danny acknowledges, however, that as he got older, his
personal prayer life was "not much to speak of." He would
pray when he was in trouble or when he needed something.
His main interest was sports. In the summer, he played
baseball and football. In the winter, he could be found in the
Catholic community center shooting baskets.

At Catholic Central High School, Danny honed his athletic skills. "I must admit that God gave me some athletic ability, especially in the area of catching a football," he says. "Because of the success I had in my junior and senior years in high school, I earned a football scholarship to Xavier University in Cincinnati."

During Danny's college years, his spiritual life began to atrophy. He continued to attend Sunday Mass — and occasionally would go to a daily Mass, especially if he had a big exam coming up. But he admits to being spiritually lax.

In the spring of his senior year at Xavier, the New Orleans Saints selected Danny in the 17th round of the NFL draft. "Since the 17th round was the very last round in the draft, I decided that I needed to work harder than I ever had in my life," he explains, "because I knew that when I reported to training camp, the coaches would be dreaming up ways to cut me from the roster."

The coaches did not cut Danny Abramowicz. In fact, by midseason he was asked to fill in as a starter because another player had been injured. During that game, he caught 12 passes against the Pittsburgh Steelers, and he remained in a starting position for the next 8 years of his career.

As a professional football player, Danny experienced success, fame, and a lot of temptations. He had married his wife, Claudia, while he was still in college, and they had started a family. But his professional life overshadowed everything. He never actually left the Church, but his spiritual life dropped further and further into the background.

"Added to all of this was a growing addiction to alcohol," Danny admits. "My conduct put a tremendous strain on my marriage. I remember waking up in the morning with a hangover, telling my wife that I was sorry and promising her that I wouldn't do it again. But lo and behold, sometimes I would be back at it again the very next day. This behavior continued even after I retired from football."

Danny's wife began to pray that God would intervene in his life. One morning, he woke up after a night of drinking, but something seemed different. He looked at his sleeping wife and then crept quietly into the bedrooms of his three children to watch them sleep. When he went into the bathroom to shave, he saw his reflection in the mirror and thought to himself: *I hate this person. And if this is the kind of life I am going to live, then life isn't worth living.*

He had hit bottom. "Here I was: a man that the world thought had it all together — a former NFL All-Pro player and an executive in the business world with all the perks. Wrong! I was miserable. I was a lost ball in the high weeds."

He went to see a Jesuit priest, who referred him to a drug- and alcohol-treatment facility, where he was asked to complete a questionnaire. Afterward, he was told that when people answer yes to two or more of the questions, they are usually on their way to becoming an alcoholic. Danny had answered yes to 14 out of 15 questions.

How Addictions Affect Faith

It's not uncommon for someone who is struggling with addictions to have a low level of spiritual or religious involvement. A close, intimate relationship with God is often impossible for addicted people because the addiction takes over their lives. It destroys their capacity for truth, sacrifice, and self-discipline. It deadens their ability to see what the addiction is doing to themselves and to the people around them. Faith in God and in other people erodes. There is no sense of inner peace. No hope. No trust. No love. Instead, an addicted person's life revolves around secrets, lies, anger, resentment, fear, and frustration.

While most people associate drugs or alcohol with addictions, there are other substances and behaviors that can destroy lives. Addictions to food, prescription drugs, gambling, shopping, sex, work, and the Internet are a few examples.

On December 15, 1981, Danny Abramowicz attended his first Alcoholics Anonymous meeting. It saved his life.

"I was not a happy camper in the early weeks of attending these meetings," he admits. "I was filled with all kinds of emotions, especially anger and feeling sorry for myself. But I kept going back and attending meetings, one day at a time. As a result, I was becoming sober, but not serene."

Danny began to feel an inner nudging that awakened in him an interest in the spiritual part of himself. He enrolled in a Bible study at a local parish. After several weeks, the instructor invited him to attend a prayer meeting. "And once again — as though somebody else inside me was answering — I said that I would attend."

Afterward, Danny was irritated at himself for saying yes, but he went to the meeting and sat in the last row. It was a Catholic charismatic group, and when people started to pray, he was shocked. People were speaking aloud words he had never heard before. Some of them were swaying and waving their hands in the air. Danny had never experienced anything like it. But then he looked around and noticed that all of the people had their eyes closed and that they were smiling. *That's what I want*, he thought to himself.

The following week he attended a Life in the Spirit Seminar. During the seminar, Danny began to see that God had not been at the center of his life. "That evening I asked the Lord, in prayer, to come into my life at the center and to change my heart," he recalls. "From that moment on, my life has never been the same."

What Is a Life in the Spirit Seminar?

A Life in the Spirit Seminar is a series of talks that helps people recognize how the Holy Spirit works in their lives and helps them make a personal commitment to Jesus Christ and the Catholic Church:

- *The **first session** is an explanation of God's love and an invitation to enter into a relationship with God.*
- *The **second session** explains the salvation offered to us through the life, death, and resurrection of Jesus, with an invitation to enter into a personal relationship with Christ.*
- *The **third session** explains how we received the gift of the Holy Spirit at our baptism and invites us to enter into a new life in the Spirit.*
- *The **fourth session** explains that when we surrender our lives to God, a burning fire enters our hearts, and a river of life flows through our souls to refresh us and sustain us.*
- *The **fifth session** helps us to pray for a full release of the Spirit in our lives so that we can use the gifts of the Spirit to help build the kingdom of God.*

- *The **sixth session** helps us to see how sin blocks the movement of the Spirit in our lives and encourages us to experience God's healing love in the Sacrament of Reconciliation.*
- *The **seventh, and last, session** invites us to grow in the Spirit through prayer, attending Mass, receiving the sacraments, reading Scripture, becoming involved in our parish community, and using our talents to serve the needs of others and to carry the Good News of Jesus Christ into the world.*

Danny was surprised to discover that after turning his life over to the Lord, things got worse for him before they got better. During his drinking days, he had made some bad financial decisions that resulted in a large debt and the possibility of losing his house. He was even more surprised that in the midst of this difficult time, the idea kept coming to him that the Lord wanted him to start a Catholic men's prayer group. He tried to ignore the idea, but it wouldn't go away. Finally, he invited 12 men to a prayer meeting. They all showed up, but none of them knew what to do, so they prayed that God would reveal His plan for them. Over time, the group grew to 90 men. "The men's prayer group was exactly what I needed at this time in my life," he admits.

It wasn't long before Danny began to realize that the same spiritual atrophy he had experienced was affecting other men. "All of this began to weigh heavily on me, so I began to pray fervently to the Holy Spirit, asking Him to help me touch men inwardly and to change their hearts," he recalls.

What came to him was the idea of using athletic terminology in a spiritual context. He started to give talks to men's groups around the country about how to become spiritually fit. People asked him if he would write a book on the topic so that they could share his insights with others. In 2004, *Spiritual Workout of a Former Saint* was published by Our Sunday Visitor.

Over the next few years, Danny's ministry to men continued to grow. In September 2008, he was invited to host the television show *Crossing the Goal* on the EWTN Catholic television network. The program uses a sports-show format to encourage men to get into "spiritual shape" by talking about relevant things that are happening in men's lives today and challenging them to do something about it. Segments include the "Kickoff," in which the problem of the day is discussed; the "Game Plan," in which facts are presented; the "Red Zone," in which the panelists talk about how they dealt with a similar problem in their own lives; and the "End Zone," which is take-away advice for the coming week.

"Guys respond to a challenge," Danny explains. "The Lord will help them, but they have to admit that something is not right in their lives."

Crossing the Goal has expanded into a broad-based evangelization ministry that includes Internet outreach, speakers at men's conferences, and leadership-training courses.

"The disease of alcoholism was the best thing that ever could have happened to me because God used it to get my attention," Danny admits. "If God can change my life around, away from the lifestyle I was living, then I think anybody has a chance of having his life changed, if he really wants to and if he is open to the prompting of the Holy Spirit."

For Additional Information

- Danny Abramowicz, *Spiritual Workout of a Former Saint* (Our Sunday Visitor, 2004).

Websites

- *Crossing the Goal*: *www.crossingthegoal.com*
- Alcoholics Anonymous: *www.aa.org*

Sally
Mews

Sally Mews has been active in evangelization and outreach to inactive Catholics since the early 1980s. She is the creator of Catholics Returning Home, a parish-based program that is used throughout the world. She came back to the Church in 1980.

SALLY MEWS grew up in a family that was scarred by alcoholism, mental illness, abuse, and poverty. As an infant, Sally was baptized into the Catholic Church, but her family rarely went to Mass. She remembers attending summer catechism classes when she was in the first or second grade, which left a lasting impression because it was the first time in her chaotic life that she actually felt God's presence.

When Sally was entering the fourth grade, the family moved to Wisconsin. Her parents enrolled Sally and her siblings in a Catholic school because it was close to home, and the children could walk to school. But her parents did not keep up with tuition payments, and they did not dress their children according to the school code. Sally remembers being reprimanded for wearing a sleeveless dress. She was afraid to walk up the aisle for Communion because her shoes were falling apart. She remembers going to school hungry — hungry not just for food, but also for the acceptance of the nuns and the other children. Her classmates called her "Sloppy Sally Sow."

"They didn't want us," Sally recalls. "We were riffraff. But I was just a little kid, and I was ostracized. I had nightmares because the nuns were always talking about going to hell. I remember telling my father we were all going to hell if we didn't go to church. So he hauled us down there one Sunday, and he went to a bar while we went to Mass."

When Sally was in the fifth grade, she discovered a chapel in a nearby Catholic hospital. She started to go to Mass there by herself. "I felt as if the Lord drew me to that chapel," she recalls. "I really didn't belong there because the Mass was intended for patients and their families. But the nuns and the chaplain at the hospital were so kind to me. They made up for the mistreatment that I experienced at school." Sally remembers praying: *I have nobody. If You're there, Lord, if You're real, I will give You my life. But I need Your help.*

By the time Sally reached the eighth grade, however, the kindness of the nuns at the hospital was not enough. She struggled to understand why the "insiders" at school, who were so obviously favored by the nuns, did not act more committed to the Lord. She became filled with anger and resentment. "I never would have imagined that I could ever stay in the Catholic Church. I had so much hurt and misinformation about what the Church was and wasn't."

Sally stopped going to Mass in her high school years. She was determined to not only survive but to succeed in life on her own. Throughout high school and college, she managed to avoid people who were drinking and doing drugs. "Alcohol had such a horrible impact on my life that I never drink whatsoever," she explains. "I never went to bars and never wanted to have anything to do with people who were into that lifestyle. Looking back, I believe the Lord protected me from all of that."

In 1968, Sally married a Protestant, who had his own painful memories of the day a Catholic boy grabbed his Bible and threw it into the wastebasket. They were married in a Catholic church because that was what was expected of them. After their son was born, they had him baptized, but they never went to Mass.

When Sally looks back, however, she sees that over the years God kept putting people on her path who would help to change her negative views. While she and her husband were students at the University of Wisconsin, for instance, she encountered former nuns who had left their vocations in the aftermath of the Second Vatican Council. "I began to see them in a different way than I did when I was a child. A lot of them were not well educated. Some of them were troubled. Some were forced to teach and should never have been in a classroom. They had large classes, and they didn't know what to do with abused children. I began to see that they were, at heart, decent people."

Sally also encountered nondenominational street preachers and people with different beliefs. A friend of her husband's kept encouraging them to join a Protestant church. Sally remembers feeling confused. She was experiencing an intense spiritual longing, but she didn't know what to do.

> ### A Spiritual Longing
>
> *Many people who have left the Church feel a deep spiritual longing. Some of the great saints have described this longing as a fire burning in their souls. Father Ronald Rolheiser, O.M.I., describes it as "a restlessness, a longing, a disquiet, a hunger, a loneliness, a growing nostalgia, a wildness that cannot be tamed, a congenital all-embracing ache that lies at the center of human experience and is the ultimate force that determines everything else."*
>
> *This spiritual longing is at the heart of what it means to be a spiritual being. The direction our lives take depends on what we do in response to our deepest spiritual desires.*

In 1979, Sally received her degree in accounting and moved with her husband and their son to a suburb of Milwaukee. She kept thinking that she had to get this religion thing figured out. She told herself that she had to do this on her own because she couldn't trust what anyone else had to say. She refused to read anything Catholic because she thought she knew everything she needed to know about the Catholic Church. Instead, she bought a Bible and began to read the Gospels.

Sally saw Jesus as a great healer, and she felt as if Jesus was trying to heal her. "I was so touched by Jesus telling the little children to come to Him. I had such a personal, overwhelming sense of how the Lord had been with me as a child. In all the bad experiences, He was there with me. I began to see that the nuns were trying to save my soul, but they just didn't know how to do it. They had no clue as to what was going on in my home life."

Sally came to the conclusion that her childhood experience of the Catholic Church had nothing to do with what Jesus is like. She began to read about other religions of the world. "I was trying to figure out what I was. I knew that I was a believer in Jesus and that I had been raised Catholic, but I wasn't sure if I could ever return to the Catholic Church. At the same time, I felt drawn to the Catholic Church. My husband thought I had flipped my lid."

One Saturday afternoon in May 1980, Sally drove around the parking lot of a nearby Catholic church, working up the nerve to go inside. When she finally entered the church, she saw a priest reading a book while he waited for people to come to confession. Sally told him her story.

"He was very nice to me," she recalls. "He helped me through my confession, and he was so touched by my sharing that he gave me the book he was reading."

Children of Alcoholics

One of the consequences for family members who have lived through the dysfunction of someone else's addiction is that they find it difficult to relate to religious symbolism that depicts God as a father or the church community as a loving and forgiving family. When they dig deeper, they often find that their feelings toward God are closely related to the problems in their families.

Sometimes the simple act of unburdening painful childhood memories in conversations with a priest (in confession), in a support group, or with a trusted friend allows people to discover that God was not the source of their pain. Sometimes, in looking back, they recognize

> *moments when God touched their lives and gave them*
> *the strength they needed to survive.*

Sally joined the parish and quickly discovered a Catholic Church that was very different from what she had experienced as a child. She enrolled her son in religious education, and she got involved in a faith-sharing group. The feeling that the Lord was leading her and preparing her for something grew stronger. She began to think about other fallen-away Catholics who might want to come back. She started to ask parish leaders about the possibility of inviting former Catholics to return, but no one seemed interested.

It wasn't until she accepted an invitation to serve on the parish finance committee that Sally faced her first crisis. "The parish had just built a new church, and they needed money," she recalls. "The committee members were talking about writing a letter to the 'deadbeats' asking them to cough up their fair share. I felt as if they were putting a knife in me. I remembered the nuns putting my name on the chalkboard because my parents didn't pay our tuition."

No one on the committee knew about Sally's childhood experiences, and they were shocked when Sally began to argue with them. She told them that this was not what Jesus would want them to do. She insisted that they had no idea what was happening in these people's lives, and that sending a letter might alienate them from the Church. She told them that if they were going to do this, they could do it without her!

In frustration, Sally wrote a letter to the Archdiocese of Milwaukee asking if something could be done to help people who were away from the Church and wanted to come back.

"I figured they would send the letter to the Vatican, and I'd be thrown out of the Church," she recalls. "But the archdiocese had just formed a committee for evangelization, and they asked me if I would be on it. I prayed about it. I thought about my son, my husband, and all of our responsibilities, but at the same time, I felt really called. I knew that something needed to be done to help all those people out there who had been told the same things I had or had been hurt or were out there thinking they are not welcome or wanted in the Catholic Church."

Before saying yes to the invitation to serve on the archdiocesan committee, Sally asked people in her prayer group to pray over her, and one of the members said: "You will be among a small group of leaders who will lead a great wave of evangelization." The words seemed overwhelming, but they proved to be prophetic. Before long, Sally was running the archdiocesan evangelization committee.

What Is Evangelization?

The word "evangelization" comes from the Greek word evangelizo, which means "to spread good news." The early Christians used the word when they spread the news about the life, death, and resurrection of Jesus Christ. Today, the Catholic Church focuses on three goals for evangelization: to renew the faith of practicing Catholics, to reach out to people who are unchurched or have fallen away from the Catholic faith, and to bring the Good News of Jesus Christ into every aspect of our modern society.

Sally's tenure on the archdiocesan evangelization committee did not last long. Within a short time, her husband was transferred to Chicago. She and her husband joined a parish in a suburb of Chicago, but they could not interest anyone in outreach to fallen-away Catholics. "No one saw the need. They would tell me that people could come back at any time. All they had to do is go to confession. But I knew that the process was much more complicated. People who had never been away from the Church themselves just didn't understand!"

Instead, they asked Sally and her husband, who had converted to Catholicism, to become leaders in the Rite of Christian Initiation of Adults (RCIA), which is the process of bringing non-Catholics into the Church. They suggested that fallen-away Catholics who wanted to come back could go through the RCIA. But Sally knew that the RCIA was not the right place for them.

A short time later, Sally and her husband moved again, and this time they were asked to coordinate the RCIA for a cluster of seven parishes. One day, a woman contacted Sally. She had seven children, and none of them went to church. She wanted to know what to do to get them to come back.

Sally took the problem to the priest in charge of the cluster, and he made her the head of an evangelization committee for the seven parishes — but the committee had a long list of things that they wanted to do, and outreach to lapsed Catholics was not on their list. One evening, before a committee meeting, the priest asked Sally to take on another project, and she broke down in tears. She told him the story of her childhood and why she felt so passionate about reaching out to other fallen-away Catholics. Stunned, he insisted that she needed to tell her story to the other members of the committee.

"So I told the group, and they all started crying," Sally recalls. "Now they finally understood, and I realized that the time had finally come for me to do something. I needed to stop doing all those other things and do what the Lord was calling me to do."

Sally put together some ideas and ran a trial program inviting fallen-away Catholics to return to one of the parishes. A deacon came to make sure she didn't say something that was incorrect. The sessions attracted a small group of people, and they all came back to the Church. Sally planned more sessions, and everything went smoothly... until a new pastor was assigned to the parish. He came unannounced to one of the sessions, and as the people began to tell their stories, he got defensive and eventually lashed out at them in anger. "He couldn't stand to hear people saying bad things about the Church," Sally explains. "The people got up and left."

Upset and frustrated, Sally called the bishop, and she received his approval to continue. He said it was clear that Sally was following God's will. So she moved the program to another parish where the pastor was supportive. Before long, word spread, and other parishes asked her to show them how they could reach out to people who were away from the Church.

After she was invited to speak at a gathering of the U.S. Catholic bishops in Washington, DC, awareness of her ministry spread throughout the country. Before long, she was receiving invitations to speak in countries all over the world. In the years that have followed, she has published several books and produced a video.

Catholics Returning Home

Catholics Returning Home is a parish-based program for helping people decide whether or not they want to return to the Catholic Church. It invites nonpracticing Catholics to attend a series of six information and faith-sharing sessions. The process allows people to explore their past experiences, their concerns, and their questions in a supportive, compassionate, and nonjudgmental way. Catholics Returning Home is usually offered in parishes three times a year — in September, in January, and after Easter — but team members are often available year-round to meet with people on an individual basis.

For additional information, call your diocesan office to find out the location of parishes in your area where this ministry is offered.

"I know firsthand what it feels like to be angry and to feel separated from the Church," Sally reflects. "I never imagined in my wildest dreams that I would ever return to the Catholic Church, much less actually end up leading a ministry to invite others back! But it's so typical of the Lord to grab someone like me by the scruff of the neck and put me into this. This is how it happened, and it still goes on. There are people out there who need this invitation. They need the Lord more than ever. And you never know what God has in mind for these people."

For Additional Information

- Sally L. Mews, *Inviting Catholics Home: A Parish Program* (Liguori, 2002).

- Sally L. Mews, *Returning Home to Your Catholic Faith: An Invitation* (Liguori, 2003).
- Sally L. Mews, *Catholics Continuing the Journey: A Faith-Sharing Program for Small Groups* (Liguori, 2006).
- Ronald Rolheiser, *The Holy Longing: The Search for a Christian Spirituality* (Doubleday, 1999).

Website

- Catholics Returning Home: *www.catholicsreturninghome.org*

Father Eduardo Montemayor, S.O.L.T.

Father Montemayor is the former director of evangelization for the Diocese of Corpus Christi, Texas. A popular speaker and workshop leader, he is currently studying for a licentiate in sacred theology (STL), with a specialization in the New Evangelization, at Sacred Heart Major Seminary in Detroit.

FATHER EDUARDO MONTEMAYOR was born on June 11, 1966, in Brownsville, Texas. The youngest of four children, he grew up crossing the border between Mexico and the United States on a daily basis.

"My mother was born in Laredo, Texas, and my father was a Mexican farmer, cattleman, and politician," he explains. "We lived in Matamoros, Mexico, where my father owned several ranches, but we went to a Catholic elementary and high school in Brownsville, which is right across the border. It was the best of both worlds!"

Eduardo spent summers at the ranch where he would ride horses, brand cattle, and talk with the cowboys. "I loved them and respected them greatly," he recalls. "But they were very poor people, and I came away from that experience with a deep love for the poor." He told his mother that when he grew up, he wanted to set aside a year of his life to help the poor.

By the time he reached his teen years, however, Eduardo became what he describes as "a materialist." When people would ask what he wanted to do when he grew up, he would tell them he wanted to be a millionaire. When they asked how he planned to do that, he would reply, "I'll do whatever it takes."

After high school, Eduardo entered Texas A&M University to study computer science. During this time, he stopped going to Mass. "When I was at home, my mother would force me to go to Mass," he recalls, "but once I went away to college, I could do whatever I wanted."

Little things kept happening, however, that he now believes were God's graces guiding and protecting him. He stopped using drugs after seeing a movie in which the parents were smoking marijuana. He remembered thinking that he wouldn't want to be a parent like that.

A little while later, he became aware of the existence of evil when a high school friend, who had joined a satanic cult, killed someone and was sentenced to life in prison. "I grew up with him," Father Eduardo recalls. "I dated his sister. If it wasn't for God's grace, I could have fallen into all of that very easily."

But the first real turning point for Eduardo happened toward the end of his second year in college when his uncle called at 2 a.m. and told Eduardo to come home immediately because his brother had been in a serious accident. Several friends offered to give Eduardo a ride to the airport, and he remembers sitting in the back seat of the car promising God that he would do anything if his brother could be okay. On the radio came the song "I Still Believe." It described being in total darkness and not knowing what to do, but the refrain was a recommitment to belief in God. The song became part of his tortured prayer.

Does God Answer Prayers?

God answers prayers, but not always in the way we might choose. If you turn to Scripture, you see that God allows bad things to happen so that something good can come from it. The most powerful example is that God did not stop the crucifixion of Jesus, but on the third day, God triumphed over death when Jesus rose on Easter Sunday. Sometimes, no matter how much we pray, we are given a cross to bear. It's never easy. But it helps if we have the faith to believe that something good will come from our pain.

When Eduardo arrived at home, he learned that his brother had died. Eduardo did not get angry at God for not answering his prayer. Instead, he felt as if God was sustaining him. During the funeral, someone handed him a rosary, and he clung to it. It was the first time he ever remembered praying the Rosary.

After Eduardo returned to school, he started going to church — not because of his mother, but because he wanted to go. "My brother's death gave me life," he recalls. "Because of my brother's death, I prayed from my heart for the first time in my life."

At the time, however, Eduardo did not realize the depths of his grief or how it was affecting him. The following week, he failed his calculus final because he couldn't concentrate. A few weeks later, Eduardo unleashed all of his raw emotions toward his sister's husband, who announced that he was leaving her for another woman. "I wanted to kill him because of the pain he caused my sister and my mother," Father Eduardo admits.

The anger inside Eduardo festered, and that summer his mother urged him to go on a silent retreat given by Father Ignacio Larrañaga, a Spanish Franciscan in El Paso. During the retreat, the priest asked Eduardo and the others to write down their hurts on pieces of paper. Then the papers were burned as a gesture of letting go of the pain. "I wrote down my brother-in-law's name," Father Eduardo says. "I remember crying. I was letting go of all the anger and hatred. I was letting go of the grief from my brother's death."

By the time Eduardo returned to college that fall, he was going to Mass regularly, but he still dreamed of becoming a millionaire. After graduation, he moved to Mexico City, where he started a business with some friends distributing suntan lotion to retail outlets in the resort cities of Mexico. His Mass attendance became sporadic again. This time the trigger that brought him back was his girlfriend's suspicion that she was pregnant. "Thank God, she wasn't," he recalls, "but it got me back to church."

Pope John Paul II's visit to Mexico City was another turning point for Eduardo. Thousands of people lined the streets, and Eduardo remembers climbing a tree so that he could see the pope. A wave of emotion passed through him as the pope went by, and Eduardo started to cry. "I went up the tree a hard-core businessman, and I came down the tree a little boy," he explains.

Eduardo began to wonder if God kept drawing him back for some purpose, but he still held to his dream of becoming a millionaire. He moved to Arizona, where he began working on a master's degree in business administration, but while there his life moved in a different direction. He joined a young-adult prayer group. He ended his relationship with his girlfriend, and he went to confession for the first time in six years. "I told the priest everything, and it was completely liberating," he recalls. "It was like I was floating!"

One day, the youth minister at his parish told him they were starting a new teen group and asked Eduardo to help. "God was moving so powerfully in me that I was literally falling in love with Jesus," he says. "I started praying the Rosary every day. I was giving talks to teenagers, and we were singing praise and worship music. It was awesome."

Today, when he looks back on this period in his life, Father Eduardo sees how much he was growing as a person. He earned his pilot's license and started a pilots' club. He became certified in scuba diving. His grades were good. In the late afternoons, he would watch the Arizona sunsets and would feel as if he could experience God in nature.

After graduating with a master's degree in 1991, Eduardo was undecided as to what to do. He still was a part owner of the suntan-lotion distributing company in Mexico, but he backed out of the company when he learned that his partners planned to distribute condoms. He found a job in

Arizona working for a large company that manufactured eyeglasses, but he had already started to wonder if he might have a vocation to the priesthood.

Where Is God Leading Me?

The term for trying to understand where God is leading us is called "discernment." It comes from the Latin word that means "to sift through."

Discernment involves prayer, reflection, writing in a spiritual journal, and setting aside quiet time for listening to what the Lord is saying. When we are trying to discern, it is a good idea to pose a question in our prayer, such as "Lord, what is it that You are asking?" Then, sit quietly, and wait for an answer. God speaks to us through ideas, inspirations, longings, and desires of the heart.

It also helps to talk about it with a priest, a deacon, or a spiritual director. Through sharing, you can often discover where you are being led.

After several months of prayer and discernment, Eduardo became increasingly convinced that God was asking him to become a priest. He called his parents to tell them. The next day his father flew to Arizona to try to talk him out of it. After three days of trying to change Eduardo's mind, his father relented. "I love you, and I respect your decision," he told Eduardo. "I will support you."

"I thanked him," Father Eduardo recalls, "and I told him that this was where I really believed God was calling me and where I would be happiest in my life."

Eduardo began to look at different religious communities. After seeing a video of Mother Teresa of Calcutta, he was captivated by her charism. In January 1993, he quit his job and applied to the Missionaries of Charity. He was accepted and officially entered in August 1993. "I gave up everything," he recalls, "and I was the happiest that I had ever been in my life. I lost my desire to be a millionaire. Nothing mattered to me except God."

Eduardo's first few years went smoothly. At the beginning of his novitiate, however, his mother was diagnosed with terminal breast cancer. Eduardo began to feel that God wanted him to go home and help his family through this ordeal. In November 1996, he asked his superior for permission to leave. The superior asked Eduardo to stay through Christmas so that he could discern a little more. "It was the most beautiful Christmas in community," he recalls. "God consoled me so much."

But on January 2, he received what he believed was a sign. His father called to tell him that his mother had taken a turn for the worst. Eduardo received permission to go home. He was determined to do whatever he could to take care of his mother. He brought her Communion every day. At night, he slept on the floor by her bed in case she needed anything.

One month later, Eduardo called his superior and told him that he was not coming back. His superior gave Eduardo his blessing, but it didn't help. Eduardo had already begun to question his faith. Here he was, in the process of giving his whole life to God, giving up everything he owned for God, and now he was asking God for one miracle — but his mother continued to get worse. He began to pray: *Lord, if You let her die, I don't know if I can love You anymore.*

His mother died at home on February 26. Eduardo was with her, and he felt an immense peace at the moment of her passing, but it was followed by feelings of intense anger at God. "At my brother's death, I was not mad at God because I was far from God," he explains. "At my mother's death, I was closer to God, and I was angry."

Two weeks after the funeral, Eduardo went on a retreat in an attempt to sort out his tortured emotions. He was still feeling conflicted when he confessed to a priest that he was angry at God.

"The priest put his arms around me and started praying," Father Eduardo recalls. "I started crying, and the more he prayed, the more I cried. At some point, I felt the anger leave me. I couldn't be angry with God anymore because I was experiencing God's love. I didn't know why my mother died, but I could not doubt God's love for me or for my mother. God's love was greater than death. I loved my mother more than anyone else in the world, but I knew now that I had been through the worst thing I could ever experience, and I came out of it with the assurance that God loved me."

When People Get Angry at God

It's important to understand that anger is an emotional response to something that we feel is unjust. It's all right to say to God, "I am angry because this person died... I am angry because You allowed this to happen... "

These emotional words are some of the best kinds of prayer because they come right from your heart. God already knows your pain. God knows how devastated you are. God loves you no matter how you feel.

*If you are angry at God, find someone that you
can talk to about your pain, and keep crying out to God
in prayer. God is the One who will ultimately help you
through whatever ordeal you are facing.*

Eduardo spent the next few months discerning what
God wanted him to do. After attending a retreat with a priest
from a religious community in Corpus Christi, Texas, he
sent a letter of inquiry asking about the possibility of entering the novitiate there. They invited him to visit. It was only
a two-and-a-half-hour drive, and during the trip, Eduardo
prayed that it would be a community that was close to Our
Lady and faithful to the Church. When he arrived, he felt as
if Our Lady were telling him: "This is where I want you."

Eduardo joined the Society of Our Lady of the Most
Holy Trinity in the summer of 1997. In June 2002, he was
ordained a priest. During his first year of priesthood, Father Eduardo fulfilled his boyhood desire to help the poor
by working with migrant farmworkers in Indiana. Then he
served as a parochial vicar at a parish in Texas, where he
started a youth group and a prayer group, and he became
involved in the charismatic renewal. In 2004, the bishop of
Corpus Christi asked him to establish an Office of Evangelization for the diocese. It was clear that evangelization
was Father Eduardo's gift. Six years later, his community
asked him to study for a licentiate in sacred theology, with
a specialization in the New Evangelization, at Sacred Heart
Major Seminary in Detroit.

"I want to do evangelization for the rest of my life," he
explains. "When I look back on my story, I see how the

Holy Spirit was working in my life. I thank God every day, and I pray that I can be an instrument of God's grace for other people."

When Father Eduardo was 16 years old, someone asked, "What do you want to be when you grow up?" He responded, "I want to be a millionaire." When he was 26 years old, he decided, by God's mercy and grace, to leave everything and follow Jesus because he had found his treasure. Today, he points to the tabernacle and says: "Jesus is my treasure. Jesus is our treasure. And you know what? Today, I can assure you that coming back to the Church and becoming a priest were wise decisions because I am happy. I am not a millionaire, but I am rich beyond my wildest dreams!"

Websites

- Missionaries of Charity Fathers: *www.mcpriests.com*
- Society of Our Lady of the Most Holy Trinity: *www.societyofourlady.net*
- The New Evangelization: *www.ewtn.com/new_evangelization/index.htm*
- Sacred Heart Major Seminary website: *www.aodonline.org/SHMS /SHMS.htm*

Dean Koontz

Dean Koontz is the critically acclaimed, best-selling author of more than 70 novels. His books have been published in 38 languages and have sold more than 400 million copies worldwide. He and his wife, Gerda, live in Southern California.

DEAN KOONTZ was born in Everett, Pennsylvania. "My mother, a fine person in so many ways, made sure that I went to church every Sunday," he recalls. "We were United Church of Christ, which was a different church then than now."

His father never attended services. "The only time he ever read the Bible or prayed, or revealed any kind of faith, was when his hard drinking, gambling, and womanizing brought him yet again to the brink of destitution," Dean remembers. "Then he made a show of reading the Bible and quoting from it. Although he never dared to say so in front of my mother, I always thought that he was an atheist."

It was during his senior year of high school that Dean first became attracted to the Catholic faith. "I began to date Gerda, whom I eventually married, and she was from a Catholic family," he explains. "Often, on a Sunday afternoon, we would drive from Bedford, Pennsylvania, the small town in which we lived, to see her aunts and uncles in Johnstown."

Dean loved those excursions. "Because of my father's alcoholism, difficulty holding jobs — he held 44 in 34 years! — and aggressively transgressive behavior, we lived in poverty, fear, and chaos," he says. "In our larger family, beyond the Koontz household, I had aunts and uncles on my mother's side, and I liked some of them very much; but too often one of them was at odds with another over some slight — real or imagined — and years would pass in which people didn't speak to each other. I never had a feeling of family in my family, never a sense of closeness and mutual love."

When Gerda and Dean visited her relatives in Johnstown, he saw a familial warmth and love that was new to him. "The members of her family seemed to care about one another in a way I'd never seen before," he recalls, "and they welcomed me so warmly that I felt as though I had long been a part of their lives. Their households were stable and full of laughter. I began to associate this sense of family and optimism with Catholicism."

When Dean went away to college, he made an effort to study Catholicism — and he found the Magisterium compelling and convincing. "Gerda never asked me to convert before marriage, but I did — and I felt at home in the Church," he recalls.

Dean never lapsed from the Catholic faith. He always believed in the promise of Christ, the truth of the Church, the Mystical Body of Christ of which we are a part, and the reality of grace in our daily lives. But the changes that came with Vatican II left him feeling that many of the bishops had lost their way and that we were being led toward something that was no longer the Church as it had been for so many centuries; that the Church was being politicized in the name of modernization; and that a drive for "social justice" and the false promise of community — rather than individual — salvation were undermining the truth of a personal God and shifting the focus from life eternal to life in the trenches of earthbound ideologies.

"To me, the utopian impulse to which so many clergymen were drawn in the late 1960s and the 1970s was scary and profane," he says. "I didn't lapse from the faith in the fullest sense, but I did lapse from confession and attendance at Mass, and became nonpracticing in that sense, though prayer remained a part of my life, and with the usual fumbling and foolishness of any human being, I tried to live by the principles of my faith."

During this time, he frequently felt as if he was being drawn back on an intellectual level. "One thing about the Catholic faith that has always appealed to me is its deep intellectual heritage, from St. Thomas Aquinas' *Summa Theologica* to the work of Christopher Dawson, G. K. Chesterton, the poetry of T. S. Eliot, and more recently the work of Richard John Neuhaus," he explains. "I continued to read in that vein, and while I felt intellectually drawn back toward the Church, I continued also to feel alienated by its march toward 'relevance,' which seemed like folly, considering that nothing could be more relevant than what it had always been before."

The impetus that finally led him back came in the form of letters from parish priests, monsignors, and even a few bishops — as well as Protestant clergymen — who recognized that his books, although spooky and sometimes humorous and sometimes disturbing, were about the eternal war between good and evil in a fallen world, about the reality of Evil with an uppercase "E," about the struggle for redemption and transcendence, about the beauty of humility, and about the ways in which we either resist grace or embrace it. Through correspondence with them, and then through a rewarding relationship with the Norbertine fathers of a local abbey, he began his return.

"I believe Pope John Paul II believed in the traditions of the Church as much as in the enduring Truth of it, and in the necessity for continuity," he admits. "Certainly, so does Pope Benedict. They, too, have brought me back toward home. I do not take this journey lightly, and it is for me all at once a spiritual, intellectual, and emotional journey that must be taken with seriousness of purpose and without any self-deception."

Changes in the Church

The Second Vatican Council (1962-1965) produced 16 documents that led to major changes in the Catholic Church. In the aftermath of the council, some people left the Church because they felt that the Church was being stripped of all that was sacred and holy. Sometimes, the changes were implemented without adequate explanation. Sometimes, priests and laypeople experimented with change in ways that were inappropriate.

Over the years, modifications have been made. Most people who return today discover that many parishes incorporate some of the rich traditions of the past into their faith communities. Eucharistic Adoration, devotions to Our Lady and the saints, Stations of the Cross, Benediction, incense, Latin hymns, and other beloved traditions can be found in many local parish communities. Most returning Catholics will tell you that it took a little getting used to, but they now like the celebration of the Mass in English, the new emphasis on Scripture, the availability of adult education, and the opportunity to get involved in parish ministries, to mention just a few of the positive changes brought about by Vatican II.

If you left the Church because of changes after the Second Vatican Council, maybe it's time to take another look.

Dean Koontz describes his decision to return to the Church as a process. "It is like writing a novel, in that the relationship with the Church and with God is the novel of my life," he explains. "I have long said that writing talent is a grace, that I did nothing to earn it and cannot therefore take pride in it. Craftsmanship is the only thing that I contribute to a novel. The rest is given to me, flows to me, quite as if from a higher power, which is in fact the case. As I write these novels, I am being shown how to write the story of my own life. When writing, I toil over each page until I can't make it better, 20 or 30 drafts, before moving on to the *next* page. Yet in spite of the difficulty of writing well, most of the moments of my life that have felt mystical have been while I am at the keyboard, crafting language, and have become aware of the presence of my Creator. Struggling toward good craftsmanship in the service of Truth is a process, and that struggle has been inextricably tied to my procession toward the Church once more."

The journey away and the journey back have had the interesting effect of relaxing the previous formality of his prayer life and making it simultaneously more casual and more intense.

"I'll give you one example, which might to some seem frivolous," he admits, "but which I assure you is not." He goes on to explain:

> Each night, when I take my dog, Anna, out for her last visit with nature for the day, when she is done, we sit on the lawn together, near the roses if they are in bloom, and watch the sunset or the stars, depending on the hour. And as I pet her, I say aloud an Our Father, a decade of Hail Marys, perhaps the Prayer to St. Michael if current circumstances seem to advise it, and then always follow with "Thank you, God, for my life, my wife, this dog, the dog who came before her, and for all those I love." Then I ask that His grace and mercy be given to those people in my life who at that moment may have health issues, emotional issues, or other problems. My dog never becomes restless during this, which does not surprise me. After all, I wrote a book — *A BIG LITTLE LIFE* — about another dog, Trixie, who I believe was a theophany, a manifestation of the divine in my life, and who had as much to do with my journey back to the Church as anything I have heretofore mentioned. Grace is everywhere, but perhaps most especially in things humble and mundane.

Website

- Dean Koontz: *www.deankoontz.com*

Deacon Waldemar Sandoval

*Wally Sandoval left the Church as a young man and
began his journey back 25 years later. He
was ordained to the permanent diaconate in 2006.*

WALLY SANDOVAL was born in Brooklyn, New York, in 1955
to a young Puerto Rican couple that had come to the United
States in pursuit of the American dream. He was part of a
large extended family that was "fiercely Catholic." When he
was very young, his aunt Esther taught him to pray, and
she instilled in him a deep desire for the things of God. She
always said that Wally was going to be a priest.

"Aunt Esther was the 'saint' in our family," he recalls.
"When I was 7, she died giving birth to her first child, and
I vowed to become a priest just as she wanted me to. From
then on, I tried never to do anything bad, always said my
prayers, and did my best in school, hoping to be the next

family saint like her. It was this desire to be perfect that would drive a wedge between me and God."

Wally became the type of child who never colored outside the lines. He did chores for the priests in the rectory and the sisters in the convent. He never spoke in class when the teacher left the room, and he always went to Mass on Sundays.

His perfect world began to crumble, however, when his parents divorced in the mid-1960s. Wally was filled with shame and tried to keep the divorce a secret. He feared that the sisters would expel him if they found out.

Keeping Secrets

An old adage warns that we are only as sick as our secrets. When we keep secrets because we are ashamed or afraid of what other people will think, we have to spend an inordinate amount of energy to keep those secrets buried beneath the surface. We live in constant fear that our secrets will be discovered. Fear begins to affect every aspect of our lives. The pressure of trying to keep secrets gives us headaches and stomachaches. It makes us feel isolated and alone. On a spiritual level, secrets destroy our relationship with God because they block God's grace from moving in our lives.

The reality is that no one is perfect. No family is perfect. God can help us through whatever difficulties we are facing, but only when we are ready to admit that we need his help. When that happens, we can join St. Paul in proclaiming, "I will all the more gladly boast of my

weaknesses, that the power of Christ may rest upon me"
(2 Corinthians 12:9).

After graduating from elementary school, Wally was accepted into a high school seminary run by the Carmelite friars in Middletown, New York. For three years, he earned top honors, was president of his class, served on the student council, and played varsity basketball. He was shocked when the rector told him at the end of his junior year that he thought Wally was not suitable for the priesthood.

"I never thought of asking if there was something I could change," he recalls. "I never thought that I could pray and ask for help. I was hurt and angry. How could the rector say that I was not a good candidate after all my efforts to do well and to be good?"

On the day Wally left the seminary in 1972, he promised God that he would still serve Him as a layperson. Back at home, he told people that he left because he needed more life experience before making a commitment to the priesthood. "So I added another secret that I needed to hide," he says.

Before long, Wally began to drift. When he was a child, everything seemed black and white. But as a young adult, he found himself in gray areas, and life became more complicated. At age 19, he fell in love with a young woman named Yolanda and her 5-month-old son. They moved in together, and several years later they had two more children of their own.

At first, Wally would go to Mass occasionally and even had the children baptized, but he and Yolanda could not be married because she had been previously married, and her husband refused to give her a divorce. Wally began to feel disconnected from God and the Church.

"I tried all kinds of diversions to fill the void," he admits. "Alcohol and substance abuse became my refuge. Miraculously, Yolanda stayed with me and prayed for me, as did my mom and many others. In my heart, I knew God loved me, but in my mind I found it impossible to reconcile my faith and my life."

The Hole in Our Souls

There's an old saying that we all have a hole in our souls that only God can fill. We may try to fill the empty spot with power, success, material possessions, drugs, or alcohol, but those things only leave us with the desire for more. It is part of our nature as spiritual beings. St. Augustine reminded us a long time ago that our souls will be restless until they rest in God.

After his second arrest for driving while intoxicated, Wally realized that he needed to return to God. "Even in this mess, God was with me," he explains. "He had not given up on me, and even now He was preparing my heart to receive Him, and my ears to hear Him."

In 1997, Wally and Yolanda began to "shop" for a church. She had grown up as a Baptist and was not comfortable with Catholicism. "I was fine with this because I thought it would be impossible for me to return to the Catholic Church anyway," Wally admits.

They decided on an Assembly of God church, with lively services and a welcoming community. "One Sunday, although no one knew me in that church, I heard my name and a voice tell me to 'get up,' the same words the Lord had spoken to the dead man in Luke's Gospel (7:14)," Wally explains. "My life was getting very complicated, and I knew I could not make it without God. I was ready to try things on His terms."

Wally approached the sanctuary during the altar call to ask God for help. When he walked out of the church that morning, something inside him was different. He had no desire to smoke or drink. His only desire was to reestablish his relationship with God. He began to read the Bible, and he started to see himself in many of the Gospel accounts. He continued to go to the Assembly of God church, but he began to feel an intense hunger for the Eucharist. At the same time, he knew that returning to the Catholic Church would mean facing his imperfections and trusting in God's mercy.

"I remembered a priest telling my mom and stepdad that they would have to live as brother and sister if they wanted to come back to the Church," he says. He feared how Yolanda would react if they were told the same thing now. He began to attend daily Mass during his lunch hour. He wondered if God was asking him to give up his relationship with Yolanda, but Yolanda was the only good thing he had in his life.

The following summer, Wally was invited to a 25th reunion at the Carmelite seminary in Middletown. He was excited about seeing old classmates but felt apprehensive about telling them he was no longer a practicing Catholic. When he was asked to do one of the readings at the Mass, he could not say no. He proclaimed the words of Galatians 4:4-6:

When the time had fully come, God sent forth his
Son, born of woman, born under the law, to redeem
those who were under the law, so that we might receive adoption as sons. And because you are sons,
God has sent the Spirit of his Son into our hearts,
crying, "Abba! Father!"

Wally felt as if God had spoken directly to him. "There
it was in black and white," he explains. "God had let me go
out from this place to try it my way, and after 25 years had
called me back to this place to tell me that He had already
freed me from the burden of my own imperfection. All I
had to do was accept what Jesus had done for me. When I
left the seminary in 1972, I didn't know how I was going to
serve the Lord, but this time I was leaving with a new hope."

That September, Wally wandered into the Church of
St. Paul the Apostle on Columbus Avenue and 60th Street
in New York City. Someone had left a book about "born-
again" Catholics in one of the pews. Wally returned it to the
bookstore in the back of the church and asked the clerk if
he could buy a copy. There were no more copies for sale,
but the clerk told Wally that he could keep this one if no one
claimed it in a week. Wally came back several times to check
on the book. At the end of the week, the clerk gave it to him.

Reading the book helped Wally to understand that true
conversion is an ongoing process of dying and rising. He
began to see that sometimes a person has to lose faith in
order to find it. A few weeks later, Wally noticed a poster
in the back of the church about a ministry called "Landings." He had earned his pilot's license some years earlier
and thought this was a ministry for people in aviation. A

closer look, however, revealed that Landings was a ministry for returning Catholics. Wally joined. After the first session, he wanted to return to the Church and asked a priest to hear his confession.

"It wasn't what I had been accustomed to as a young boy," he explains. "No dark confessional, no laundry list of sins. It was warmer, friendlier, more like a conversation, even though I was the only one talking most of the time. When I finished, the priest assured me that God was at work in my life — and although I had abandoned God, He had never given up on me. If I was ready to trust in Him and work with Him, God would overcome all the obstacles I had put between us. The priest said transformation doesn't happen all at once but little by little, much the same way I had drifted away."

The first person Wally wanted to tell about his decision to come back to the Catholic Church was his mother. She and his stepfather had returned to the Church years earlier. She had been praying for Wally and had given him some tapes from a retreat she had attended, but Wally had never listened to them. He decided to play the tapes before calling her. The topic was forgiveness, and as he listened, resentments from the past began to float up and pop like bubbles in the air.

He called his mother and blurted out, "Mom, I forgive you."

"For what?" she asked.

"For everything," he said, with the hope that it wouldn't be necessary to explain that he was referring to the divorce so many years before.

After a short pause, his mother said, "I forgive you too."

"For what?" Wally asked.

"For everything," she said, and they both laughed.

The Healing Power of Forgiveness

Most people who feel drawn back to the Catholic Church discover that part of the process involves forgiving other people — and in some cases, forgiving themselves. Forgiveness allows resentment to drain out of our souls so that we can be more open to God's love. We begin by expressing our desire to forgive, and we ask the Lord to help us let go of the pain, the anger, and any negative feelings we may be holding on to. The healing that comes from forgiveness is a gift from God. It brings a deep inner peace that allows us to see our situation from a different perspective.

In the months that followed, Wally became more involved at St. Paul's, and one Sunday he asked Yolanda if she would come with him. "It happened to be Black History Month," Wally recalls. "A choir from Harlem sang gospel-style songs, and a charismatic priest preached like a Pentecostal minister. Needless to say, my wife was impressed."

After Mass, Yolanda agreed to stop by a parish event in the auditorium. On the way down the steps, she found a $20 bill. "See what a wonderful church this is," Wally said. "At most churches, you give money to God; but here, God gives money to you!"

Wally was secretly hoping Yolanda would become a Catholic, but he was afraid to mention it. On their way home, they arrived at the subway station and saw a homeless man rummaging through a garbage can. Yolanda reached into her pocket and gave him the $20 bill she had found at St. Paul's.

"God bless you, lady! Hallelujah! God is good!" the man shouted.

Wally stood dumbfounded. He had brought Yolanda to St. Paul's to show her something about his faith, and with one small gesture, she showed him that her faith was just as strong.

Wally and Yolanda became involved in the liturgies, ministries, and service opportunities at St. Paul's. After Wally had shared his personal testimony at a parish retreat, one of the priests asked him if he had ever considered becoming a deacon. Wally explained that Yolanda had been married before and that they were still not legally husband and wife. The priest offered to help. Arrangements were made for Yolanda to get a divorce. Then the priest helped Yolanda have her first marriage annulled by the diocesan tribunal. After receiving the decree of nullity, Wally and Yolanda were married at St. Paul's — and two years later, Wally was accepted into the diaconate-formation program.

The Permanent Diaconate

In the early Church, married men were ordained as deacons for the purpose of caring for widows and helping to serve the physical needs of the growing Church. In 1967, Pope Paul VI restored the permanent diaconate, allowing married men (aged 35 and older) to be ordained as deacons. Their responsibilities include preaching and teaching, baptizing, witnessing marriages, conducting wake and funeral services, and leading prayer services. They also maintain their original mandate of serving those in need.

The call to the diaconate is considered to be a vocation. Preparation for the diaconate includes spiritual formation and formal studies in philosophy, theology, and pastoral ministry. Deacons receive the Sacrament of Holy Orders. They are not allowed to hear confessions and give absolution, anoint the sick, or celebrate Mass.

"There were many trials along the way," Wally admits, "like cancer and diabetes and the death of my father, all while I was trying to get through the deaconate-formation program. But this time, I was relying, not on my own strength or faith, but on Christ."

On June 9, 2006, Wally was ordained a permanent deacon for the Archdiocese of New York, and he was assigned to serve at St. Paul the Apostle Parish in Manhattan, where he visits the sick and the homebound, conducts baptismal classes, celebrates infant baptisms, and serves on several parish committees. He also leads the Landings program and helps other people, like himself, return to the Catholic Church.

Yolanda eventually decided to become a Catholic. "I tell her that we are an example of where the Church needs to be — accepting our diversity, supporting one another, and continuing the conversion process through dialogue and charity," he explains.

Deacon Wally Sandoval admits that there are times when he still feels fearful and full of doubts. "People who are in the Church are not so different from those that are lapsed," he admits. "We are all frightened and fail to exercise our faith at times. But Christ continues inviting us to accept His mercy, giving us the necessary grace to face our fears, our weaknesses and our strengths, our joy and our sorrow, continuously nourishing us with His Body and transforming us into a Eucharistic community."

What Is "Landings"?

"Landings" is a ministry that was established for Catholics who have drifted away from the Church. Each group is no larger than 10 or 12 people. They meet for 10 weeks. They pray together, listen compassionately to one another's stories, and then dialogue with one another about some of the issues that keep people away or draw them back to God and His Church. They do not argue or attempt to teach. There is no obligation to return to the Church, and there is no charge.

Many who come to Landings find their way back to a fuller participation in the Church and a deeper commitment to Christian living through involvement in ministry or further study. The main purpose of each group is to provide a safe environment in which people can explore their own potential for growth in their relationship with God.

Websites

- Landings International: *www.paulist.org/landings*
- Church of St. Paul the Apostle: *www.stpaultheapostle.org*

Janet Morana

Janet Morana serves as the executive director of Priests for Life and the cofounder of the Silent No More Awareness Campaign, the world's largest mobilization of women and men who have lost children to abortion.

JANET MORANA was born into a Catholic family in Brooklyn, New York. She grew up going to confession on Saturday afternoons, attending Mass the following morning, and then gathering together with family members for Sunday dinner. She remembers the Latin Mass in the pre-Vatican II Church and the mystical elements that surrounded the liturgy. "You felt as if you were entering into the presence of God," she recalls.

Janet also remembers feeling lost and confused when the Mass changed in the aftermath of the Second Vatican Council. "The priest turned around, the Mass was in English, there was no more incense, and the organ music was replaced by guitars and tambourines."

Standing in line for confession one day at her Catholic high school, Janet suddenly decided: *I'm not going to do this anymore! I don't even know what I believe, and I'm not going to do this!* From that moment on, Janet stopped going to confession. It wasn't long before she started skipping Mass. "You stop doing this, and then you stop doing that, and before you know it, you're not a practicing Catholic anymore," she explains.

Janet went on to earn an undergraduate degree in foreign languages, a master's degree in education, and a professional diploma in reading. She married and lived with her husband's parents in a two-family home on Staten Island, where she worked as a substitute teacher.

After her three daughters were born, Janet let her in-laws take the children to church, using the "excuse" that she had to stay home and get ready for Sunday dinner. Two days before Christmas in 1988, Janet landed the full-time teaching position that she had been hoping to get. Her mother-in-law was praying a novena for Janet to get the teaching position, which Janet had dismissed — as if this could help get her the job! Now her mother-in-law told her that she should go to church and light a candle in thanksgiving.

Janet was so happy about the job that she did what her mother-in-law asked and went to light a candle. It was the first time she had been alone in a church in a long time, and while she was there she decided that maybe the time had come for her to start going to Mass with her daughters.

The following weekend, Janet went to Mass, but she refused to receive Communion because she still did not believe in confession. Her daughters noticed and decided to do something about it. After Mass one Sunday, they dragged Janet over to meet the newly ordained Father Frank Pavone, who had been assigned to the parish a short time earlier.

"Father Frank, this is my mother, the one I told you needed to go to confession," her daughter Tara Lynn announced.

Janet blushed. Father Pavone smiled and said: "Very pleased to meet you! Don't worry. You don't have to go to confession. But if you want, you can come and talk to me sometime."

There was something about the invitation that intrigued Janet. When she called, Father Pavone invited her to meet him at the rectory. She was nervous, but he put her at ease by asking about her background. Then he said, "What do you think is keeping you from going to confession?"

"I disagree with the teachings of the Church," she replied.

When Father Pavone asked which teachings were causing the problem, Janet starting going through a list that included papal infallibility, birth control, and of course, the need to tell your sins to a priest!

Father Pavone suggested that they begin by looking at some of the Church documents that explain these teachings. "If you're willing to read, we can talk about it," he said. "You can tell me your objections, and we can discuss them."

When People Disagree With the Church

It's not unusual for people to say that they struggle with some of the teachings of the Catholic Church. Often their opinions are based on things that they read or heard in the secular media, which don't provide a full explanation for a particular teaching. It's important to understand that Catholic teaching always comes from God speaking through Scripture, Tradition, natural law, and the authority of the pope and the bishops to formulate Catholic teaching based on how divine revelation applies in society today.

For example, the Church interprets the Fifth Commandment — "Thou shalt not kill" — as a prohibition against homicide, euthanasia, suicide, and abortion, with strong warnings that the death penalty and war are allowable only in extreme cases. As new technologies develop, the Church tries to apply the teachings of the Gospel to ethical concerns, such as the moral ramifications of organ transplants, do-not-resuscitate orders, feeding tubes, physician-assisted suicide, in vitro fertilization, stem cell research, and genetic engineering.

Before you decide to disagree with Church teaching, it is important to find out exactly what the Church teaches and why. Many people who feel as if they are being drawn back to the Church, but struggle with Church positions on various issues, are encouraged to go with the movement of God's grace. They sometimes acquire a new and deeper understanding when they look at the issues from a faith perspective. Or they discover that their doubts and disagreements are resolved as they experience spiritual healing and a profound change of heart.

It took four months of reading and talking before Janet began to feel that she wanted to go to confession. "I had to work through all my 'problems' and my 'points,'" she explains. But after finally receiving the Sacrament of Reconciliation one Saturday evening after Mass, she was astounded. "It just felt so good! I could feel a weight coming off, and it was such a warm feeling."

After confession, Janet told Father Pavone that she was looking forward to receiving Communion the next morning when she came to Mass with her children. But Father Pavone said, "Why wait until tomorrow? I can give you Communion right now!" So she knelt by the tabernacle, and when he placed the consecrated host on her tongue, she knew that Jesus was with her.

"I really felt that this was my first Communion," she says. "It's just hard to describe how I felt. It was peace and warmth, and I knew that I was with Jesus."

Janet began to get involved in parish activities. In October 1990, she attended her first prayer vigil at an abortion clinic. During the demonstration, she had the opportunity to talk with several women who had come to the clinic for an abortion. One young woman agreed to talk with the counselors at the pregnancy center. Janet was convinced that a baby had been saved.

"It was like a steel door dropped behind me that day, and from that point forward, my passion to do something about abortion became so intense that I knew I had to commit myself to this work," she explains.

Three years later, with the permission of Cardinal John O'Connor, Father Pavone left the parish and became the first full-time national director of Priests for Life. Janet was teaching full-time but volunteered to help in her free time. In the beginning, they shipped all of the Priests for Life information and resources from Janet's basement.

As the movement grew, Janet knew that she had to make a choice. In 2000, she gave up her teaching position to work full-time with Father Pavone. Once the decision was made, she felt an overwhelming sense of peace, and she was convinced that she had done the right thing.

In 2003, Janet and Georgette Forney became cofounders of the Silent No More Awareness Campaign, which educates the public about the damage to women and men caused by abortion. "Georgette herself had had an abortion," Janet explains, "and she was convinced that there were other women out there who were willing to tell the story of how abortion had hurt them."

Powerful testimonies began to pour in. Women offered to tell their stories at meetings and conferences. They began to spread the message that abortion is not an unforgivable sin. They offer hope and healing to women who are suffering from past abortions.

Post-Abortion Syndrome

Society recognizes the need for women to grieve and heal after a miscarriage or a stillbirth. But few recognize that women who have had abortions experience a variety of emotional difficulties. Experts now recognize that depression, feelings of worthlessness and alienation, guilt, shame, anger, difficulty concentrating, sleep disorders, and anxiety can occur. Many women feel separated from God and are unsure if they can ever be forgiven for what they did.

What they need to know is that forgiveness — the forgiveness of God and the ability to forgive themselves — is what will help them begin the healing process. If you

> or someone you know is struggling with emotional tur-
> moil after having an abortion, it is important to get help.
> If you want anonymity, call your diocesan office and ask
> for information.

In addition, members of the Silent No More Awareness Campaign try to reach women who are considering an abortion, in the hope that sharing their insights and experiences will help these women make the right decision. They also hope that their message will reach people who are unaware of how abortion hurts the baby, the mother, and society as a whole.

"We want people who are conflicted in their attitudes toward abortion to hear the stories of women and say to themselves, 'Ah, abortion isn't good for women after all!' " Janet explains.

Since coming back to the Church, Janet has held various local and national leadership roles in the pro-life movement. She has traveled extensively throughout the United States and around the world giving talks and offering pro-life training seminars. She has coordinated relationships between pro-life organizations, the Vatican, and the United States government. She is the cohost and producer of the *Gospel of Life* series seen on the Catholic Familyland Television Network and the multidenominational NRB Network. She is a frequent guest on Teresa Tomeo's *Catholic Connection* radio show, heard on EWTN Radio worldwide.

In 2009, the international Legatus organization bestowed upon Janet the Cardinal John J. O'Connor Pro-Life Award. She is featured on Father Pavone's *Defending*

Life television series on EWTN, and beginning in the spring of 2011 Janet will cohost, with Teresa Tomeo, a brand-new miniseries called *The Catholic View for Women*.

Janet's advice for people who have family members or friends who are away from the Church is simple and straightforward: "Follow my mother-in-law's example," Janet says. "She never badgered me about not going to church but was a great witness to her Catholic faith. As a daily communicant, she prayed for me, so that I would return to the faith."

As for Janet's own experience of coming back, she says:

> I now know how rich our Catholic Church is in its teaching and legacy. I know what it means to read the Bible and have a real relationship with Jesus Christ. Grace is always there for us. We must open our hearts to receive it. I feel blessed to be back in full communion with the Catholic Church.

For Additional Information

- "Catholic 'Revert' Silent No More," by Tom McFeely, *National Catholic Register* (August 26-September 1 issue, 2007).

Websites

- Priests for Life: *www.priestsforlife.org*
- Silent No More Awareness Campaign: *www.silentnomoreawareness.org*

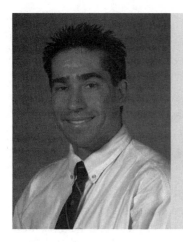

Dr. Francis Beckwith

Dr. Beckwith is a professor of philosophy and church-state studies at Baylor University, and a fellow and resident scholar at Baylor's Institute for Studies of Religion. He has published numerous books and articles. He was the president of the Evangelical Theological Society when he made the decision to return to the Catholic Church in 2007.

FRANCIS "FRANK" BECKWITH was born in 1960 into a large Catholic family in Brooklyn, New York. His family was an eclectic mix of mostly Italian Americans and others of French-Canadian and English descent. When he was 6 years old, the family moved to Las Vegas, where his father worked as an accountant and internal auditor at several hotels.

Frank was the oldest of the four Beckwith children, and their parents kept a close watch on them in what was commonly known as "Sin City." They went to Mass every Sunday, and the children all went to Catholic schools. "I was part of the first generation of American Catholics who would have no memory of the Church prior to Vatican II," he explains. "This meant that I grew up and attended Catholic schools during a time in which well-meaning Catholic leaders were testing all sorts of innovations in the Church, many of which were deleterious to the proper formation of young people."

Frank remembers that while serving as an altar boy, some of the priests were excited about the changes in the Church, and others were annoyed. He was confirmed when he was in the seventh grade and soon afterward became fascinated with Jesus. He remembers having a dream about Jesus one night. "We were sitting, facing each other, with the landscape of heaven in the background," he recalls. "He spoke to me."

The next morning, Frank woke up and found a copy of the New Testament that a friend of his father's had left on the kitchen table the night before. He started to read the Bible and was so taken by the person of Christ that he made a personal commitment to live by Jesus' teachings.

"I recall one incident in which a bully at school punched me during recess," he admits. "I literally turned the other cheek and offered it to him for a second punch. He freaked out and told me I was weird. The other students did not know what to make of me."

The next time his father's friend came to visit, Frank asked him about Jesus. The man invited Frank to Maranatha House, a nondenominational ministry run by hippies who had embraced the Jesus movement in the 1970s. At

Maranatha House, Frank was exposed to Scripture study, dynamic teachings, Christian music, and a variety of books and tapes by prominent Protestant theologians. It was like nothing he had ever experienced in the Catholic Church or at his Catholic school.

Frank admits that he quickly became a bit of a "know-it-all," who readily quoted Scripture passages and challenged family members and friends about their faith. At a mission given by Dominican priests at his parish, he grilled the priests with questions that were peppered with the same Scripture quotes he had heard at Maranatha House. One of the Dominicans warned him that biblical passages must be read in context. As an example, the priest quoted a passage from Psalm 14 that reads, "There is no God," and pointed out to Frank that if you take that passage out of context, you could argue that the Bible teaches atheism. The priest went on to explain that the complete passage reads: "The fool says in his heart, 'There is no God'" (Psalm 14:1).

It was an important lesson for Frank, but it did not draw him back to his Catholic roots. In fact, he became even more immersed in the welcoming community and Scripture study at Maranatha House.

In 1974, Frank graduated from elementary school and entered Bishop Gorman High School. During his freshman year, he drifted away from Maranatha House. He was still going to Mass every Sunday with his parents, but during his sophomore year he began to have doubts about his faith. He considered himself an agnostic. Religion classes in high school did nothing to restore his faith.

In the spring semester of his senior year, he became depressed for no apparent reason, and he began to wonder if his unhappiness stemmed from his skepticism about faith. One afternoon, he knelt next to his bed and asked God to help him. There was a radio on his dresser set to a rock station. But at that moment, a Christian station cut in, and the disc jockey talked about committing one's life to Christ. "I later learned from a friend that what happened to my FM radio is a naturally explicable phenomenon that sometimes occurs," he explains. "But given the timing and content of my prayer, the radio stations involved, and the DJ's message, I have never ceased to think of that incident as a gentle tap on my shoulder from the Lord, who knew that I had never really stopped believing in Him."

Unsure of what to do next, Frank called the friend of his father who had taken him to Maranatha House five years earlier. The man put him in contact with a local high school teacher, who invited Frank to a Bible study and eventually led him to the Neighborhood Foursquare Church.

After graduating from high school, Frank entered the University of Nevada at Las Vegas with the plan to major in journalism. In February of his freshman year, he broke his ankle. While he was recuperating, he read books on philosophy, theology, and history. After he recovered, he started attending Protestant lectures and became more deeply immersed in evangelical Protestant beliefs.

Frank no longer thought of himself as a Catholic; he considered himself a committed Protestant. By his junior year, thinking he was being called to the ministry, he switched his major to philosophy, which would prepare him for the study of apologetics, to defend the truths of Christianity.

> ### What Is "Apologetics"?
>
> *"Apologetics" is a term used for efforts to explain the Christian faith. Both Catholic and Protestant scholars engage in apologetics. For Catholics who are interested in apologetics, emphasis is placed on scriptural, historical, traditional, and rational grounds for Catholic teaching. One of the most active authors of Catholic apologetics is Karl Keating and his Catholic Answers publications. You can find books on apologetics in Catholic bookstores or libraries. If you have Internet access, check out Catholic apologetics websites.*

During his senior year in college, Frank talked with a Christian apologist who urged him to enroll in a new Christian school in Southern California, where he would be exposed to a wider variety of Protestant beliefs and traditions. That fall, Frank entered Simon Greenleaf University, where he earned a master's degree in Christian apologetics. Unlike many of the students who had negative reactions to anything Catholic, Frank believed that he could gain valuable insights from Catholic theologians, and it was during this time that he began to read G. K. Chesterton and St. Thomas Aquinas. It wasn't long before he realized that he would have to earn a Ph.D. in philosophy if he really wanted to pursue a career as an academic.

Frank's mother suggested that he apply to Fordham, a Jesuit university in New York City, where he could live with his grandmother while going to school. She probably hoped that exposure to his Catholic grandmother and the Jesuits might bring him back to the Church, but it did not work out that way. Frank was accepted, and he studied under some of the finest Catholic philosophical minds in the country. But he maintained contact with evangelical scholars, and he viewed everything he learned from a Protestant perspective.

"My studies at Fordham helped form and shape my views on God's nature, the human person, and the natural moral law," Frank explains. "But none of these views seemed to me at the time inconsistent with Protestant theology, as the works of some Thomistic and Thomas-friendly evangelical Protestant thinkers clearly showed."

During the summer of 1985, when Frank returned to Las Vegas for summer vacation, he became reacquainted with Frankie, the woman who would become his wife. They both attended Vineyard Christian Fellowship. By the following summer, they were engaged, and they married in the summer of 1987. Two years later, Frank accepted a faculty appointment in the Philosophy Department at the University of Nevada at Las Vegas.

In 1996, he moved to Whittier College in Southern California for a short time, and he eventually accepted a position at Trinity International University's California campus. During this time, he became an ordained minister of United Evangelical Churches — but ironically, he and his wife felt drawn to an Episcopal church. His wife commented that the liturgies at the Episcopal church seemed very much like the Catholic Masses they had attended with the Beckwith family members. "But I had theological problems with Catholicism," Frank explained. "My reasons included justification, the Eucharist, and the papacy."

What Catholics Believe

There are many misconceptions over what Catholics believe. Here are a few:

- ***Justification.*** *Many Protestants accuse Catholics of trying to earn salvation by performing good deeds. They believe in justification by faith alone. The Catholic belief in justification is that we are saved by God's grace, which we receive at Baptism, when we die to sin and arise as a new creation in Christ. But Catholics also believe that by our baptism, we are called to live the Gospel message in our words and in our actions.*
- ***The Eucharist.*** *Many Protestants celebrate communion services as a remembrance of the Last Supper and think of communion as a symbol. Catholics believe that during the Mass, the bread and wine are changed into the Body and Blood of Jesus Christ. When we receive Communion, it is more than a symbol. It is the Body, Blood, Soul, and Divinity of Jesus Christ.*
- ***The papacy.*** *Many Protestants do not recognize the teaching authority of the pope. Catholics believe that throughout the centuries, there has been an unbroken line of popes who are successors to St. Peter, with each one serving as the Vicar of Christ and leader of the universal Church on earth.*

In 2000, Frank spent a year in St. Louis, where he earned a master of juridical studies degree at Washington University School of Law. He returned to Trinity for a

165

year and then received a full-time faculty appointment at Princeton during the 2002-2003 school year. While he was there, he reconnected with Hadley Arkes, a legal philosopher from Amherst College, who bluntly asked him one day, "Why are you a Protestant rather than a Catholic? Didn't you grow up Catholic?"

The question stunned Frank — especially since Hadley Arkes was Jewish! "I gave him the standard Protestant theological responses — ones that I firmly believed were adequate for the task at hand."

But Hadley was not satisfied. "That's all?" he asked. "That's it? You were brought up Catholic. Your parents are Catholic. I don't see why you don't return to the Church."

It was the first time anyone outside Dr. Beckwith's family had ever asked him about returning to the Catholic Church, but it would not be the last.

In 2003, Frank and Frankie Beckwith moved to Texas, where Frank accepted a tenure-track position at Baylor University. Almost immediately, he experienced controversies at Baylor that centered on his theological views. During the next few years, several unrelated incidents would challenge his beliefs even more.

It started with a telephone call from his 8-year-old niece, Darby, asking why he wasn't a Catholic. He told her that he respected the Catholic Church but disagreed with some things. "Okay," she replied. "I understand. But I am still sad. We will pray for you."

"This encounter with my niece marked the first step in our movement toward the Catholic Church," he admits. "It seemed not to be such a big deal at the time. After all, this was an 8-year-old child unacquainted with the serious theological questions for whom someone in my line of work requires answers. Although that may be true, beneath Darby's inquiry was a more fundamental question, one for which I should have had an answer: 'Can I give a convincing account as to why I should permanently abandon the Church of my baptism?' "

The next incident took place in February 2006 at a theology conference hosted by Boston College. Dr. Beckwith delivered a paper. He argued that Protestants — many of whom don't believe that creeds (such as the Apostles' Creed and the Nicene Creed) are necessary — embrace doctrines they claim are unassailable. He pointed out that many anti-creed Protestants believe in the Trinity and other elements of Christian faith that are not directly supported in Scripture but were passed on during the first six centuries of Christianity.

What Are Creeds?

Creeds are statements of belief that were developed by the early Church. The Apostles' Creed was compiled around 150 years after the apostles died. It is called the "Apostles' Creed" because it summarizes what the apostles taught.

The Nicene Creed was composed in A.D. 325 during the Council of Nicaea, which was convened by Emperor Constantine in an attempt to unify all of the early Christians with one doctrine of the Trinity and one understanding of the divinity and humanity of Jesus Christ. Today, we recite the Nicene Creed during Mass as a common declaration of our faith.

During the question-and-answer period, a Boston College philosophy professor (who had converted to Catholicism from evangelical Protestantism while in graduate school) asked Frank why he wasn't Catholic if he espoused this opinion about the creeds. The question thrust him into doing additional research so that he could justify why he was not a Catholic. He began reading the work of Cardinal Joseph Ratzinger, who would become Pope Benedict XVI. He also began to read books by evangelicals who had converted to Catholicism.

One month after the Boston College conference, Dr. Beckwith was denied tenure at Baylor University. He appealed the decision, and the next few months were filled with tension on both a personal and a professional level.

Six weeks after his tenure denial, Frank's father-in-law died. In going through her father's personal belongings, Frankie found a St. Christopher medal that had been given to her father by a Bishop Choi during World War II. Frankie's father had wanted to become a Catholic, but his wife had discouraged him. After that, he never participated in any church — not even the Protestant church that his wife and daughters attended.

Frankie became concerned over whether her father had been "saved," because to her knowledge, other than his desire to become a Catholic, he had never made a commitment to Jesus Christ or to the Christian faith. A friend reassured her that the Catholic Church would consider him "baptized by desire" and that God would honor his act of faith. "This gave Frankie much comfort," Frank recalled.

Who Is Saved?

Most Catholics aren't sure what to say when someone begins asking whether or not someone is "saved." Catholics believe that salvation comes through Jesus Christ. Jesus died for our sins and redeemed the human race. We believe that in the Sacrament of Baptism, we are "reborn of water and the Spirit" (CCC, 1257). The Church teaches that Baptism is necessary for salvation.

But the Catechism of the Catholic Church (nn. 1258 and 1259) explains that the Church also holds that those who die for the faith without being baptized and those who wanted to be baptized but died before receiving the sacrament are saved.

Catholics also believe that people can freely accept or reject the gift of salvation. A person's commitment to Christ is not a onetime event. Catholics see conversion and commitment to Christ as an ongoing process that draws them into closer union with God throughout their lives.

In September 2006, after a six-month battle, Frank finally received tenure. Sixteen months later, he was promoted to full professor. "In the academic world, such a story is as unlikely as they come," he admits. "For this reason, I am in awe of, and humbled by, the gentle and unpredictable hand of Providence that has taken my wife and me by its grace through one improbable scenario after another."

The following month, Frank and Frankie Beckwith had breakfast with friends from the University of Texas in Austin who had become Catholic three years earlier. They spent the next three hours talking about the Catholic faith. Frank recalls:

> Our questions focused on several theological issues that prevented us from becoming Catholic and seemed insurmountable: the doctrine of justification, the Real Presence in the Eucharist, the teaching authority of the Church (including apostolic succession and the primacy of the pope), and [the Sacrament of] Penance. The other issues that most Protestants find to be stumbling blocks — the Marian doctrines and purgatory — were not a big deal to me. That was because I reasoned that if the Catholic views on Church authority, justification, the Communion of Saints, and the sacraments were defensible, then these other so-called stumbling blocks withered away, since the Catholic Church would in fact be God's authoritative instrument in the development of Christian doctrine.

His friends encouraged him to read the Church Fathers and the *Catechism of the Catholic Church*. It was several months before Frank would follow their advice. In the meantime, he was elected the 58th president of the Evangelical Theological Society, a professional, academic society with more than 4,500 scriptural scholars, teachers, pastors, students, and others involved in evangelical scholarship.

Catechism of the Catholic Church

During the Synod of Bishops in 1985, a request was made for the development of a catechism that would include all

of Catholic doctrine regarding faith and morals. The fol-
lowing year, Pope John Paul II established a commission of
cardinals and bishops, and he gave them the task of draft-
ing a catechism. The effort took six years, and on June 25,
1992, Pope John Paul II approved the text. In his apostolic
constitution Fidei Depositum, *the Holy Father called the*
Catechism *"a statement of the Church's faith and of catho-*
lic doctrine, attested to or illumined by Sacred Scripture,
the Apostolic Tradition, and the Church's Magisterium."

The pope declared that the Catechism *would be the*
norm for teaching the faith. He hoped that it would help
to renew the Church and deepen the faith of Catholics.

Today, the Catechism of the Catholic Church *is avail-*
able in hardcover, paperback, and online versions. It is a
wonderful resource for anyone who wants to know more
about the Catholic faith.

By early 2007, Frank had started to read many of the books his friends had recommended, and his attraction to the Catholic Church grew stronger. "I became convinced that the early Church is more Catholic than Protestant and that the Catholic view of justification, correctly understood, is biblically and historically defensible," he explains.

He reached the conclusion that the Catholic Church was indeed the church that Christ had established. Ironically, his wife, Frankie, had come to the same conclusion, for her own very different reasons, a little while earlier. On March 23, 2007, Frank and Frankie Beckwith met with a priest and told him about their desire to seek full communion with the Catholic Church.

Because Frank was still the president of the Evangelical Theological Society, several friends had advised him not to return to the Catholic Church until his term ended in November. They wanted his decision to attract as little attention as possible.

Unsure of what to do, Frank and Frankie Beckwith prayed for guidance. On the morning of April 20, they felt as if they received a sign. Frank's 16-year-old nephew, Dean, called and said he would be receiving the Sacrament of Confirmation on May 13. Several months earlier, Frank had written a long letter to Dean affirming the importance of the sacrament and encouraging him to do his best to prepare himself spiritually. The letter was followed by some serious conversations between uncle and nephew about faith. Dean insisted that because of Frank, his faith in Christ had been renewed. He wanted Frank to be his confirmation sponsor. But Frank could only do that if he came back to the Church.

A few days before returning to the Catholic Church, Frank resigned his ordination with the United Evangelical Churches. On Saturday, April 28, 2007, he went to St. Jerome Catholic Church in Waco, Texas, to receive the Sacrament of Reconciliation for the first time in more than 30 years. He entered the confessional and sat face-to-face with the priest.

"Father, forgive me, for I have sinned," he began. "It has been over 30 years since my last confession. I'm not sure I can remember all of my sins."

"That is all right," the priest replied. "God knows them all."

Then the priest heard his confession and gave him absolution. The next morning, Frank Beckwith was publicly received back into the Catholic Church at the 11 a.m. Mass. His wife was accepted as a candidate for full communion with the Church.

On May 5, 2007, Frank resigned as president of the Evangelical Theological Society, and two days later he resigned as a member of the group. "I did not want my return to the Catholic Church to cause needless offense to my brothers and sisters in Christ from whom I had learned so much in my over three decades in the Protestant world," he explains.

After Dr. Beckwith's resignation, the executive committee issued a press release explaining why a Catholic could not be a member. One of Frank's former colleagues warned that he was "embracing serious theological error." As news of his return to the Catholic Church spread, Frank received hundreds of e-mails —both supportive and condemning.

"My return to the Catholic Church had as much to do with a yearning for a deeper spiritual life as it did with theological reasoning," he admits. He adds:

> Since becoming Catholic, I have become much more prayerful, I read the Bible far more often, and I am increasingly more aware and appreciative of the grace God has given me to live a virtuous life. I sometimes find myself silently praying a Hail Mary or an Our Father while driving or working out. I am not averse to asking particular saints to pray for me or to recite the prayers of some favorite saints, such as Thomas Aquinas. When doing this I gain a greater sense of that of which I am a part, the wonderful Body of Christ that transcends time, space, and death itself.

Dr. Beckwith's wife, Frankie, was received into the Church on August 18, 2007. Frank is still a professor at Baylor University. He and Frankie are parishioners of St. Joseph Catholic Church in Bellmead, Texas.

For Additional Information

- Francis J. Beckwith, *Return to Rome: Confessions of an Evangelical Catholic* (Brazos Press, 2009).

Websites

- Francis Beckwith: *www.francisbeckwith.com*
- Francis Beckwith blog: *www.patheos.com/community/returntorome*

Barbara Curtis

Barbara Curtis is a wife, the mother of 12 children, the grandmother of 12, and the author of over 1,200 articles and 9 books. In her "Mommy Life" blog, she offers parenting, cultural, political, and spiritual insights. She lives in northern Virginia with her husband, Tripp, their four sons with Down's syndrome, and their daughter, Maddy.

BARBARA CURTIS was baptized in the Catholic Church but was not raised as a Catholic. "By the time I was 6, we had lived in eight different states, because my father was always on the run from creditors," she explains. "I went to Catholic school in the first grade and received my First Communion, but then my father left my mother, me, and my two brothers."

Barbara's mother moved to Washington, DC, and put the children into a foster home in Maryland. "It was a very

175

abusive situation," Barbara recalls. "My brothers and I were all molested by the father, and I was raped by the teenage son."

Barbara's mother eventually brought the children back to live with her in a one-bedroom apartment. "She would leave before we got up in the morning and come home after we were in bed," Barbara explains. "She was working two or three jobs to support us, but she also had problems with alcohol and men. I don't remember my mom ever talking about Jesus or God, or reading to us. My mother was always bitter and angry toward the Catholic Church."

At school, Barbara was one of only two white children in her class. "My role models of good families were the black families who were our neighbors," she recalls. "They were poor, but they had their dads at home, and they always said grace at dinner. They gave me a vision of what a family should be."

When Children Grow Up With Bad Role Models

Children learn by watching the adults in their lives. They learn about love by being loved. They learn about forgiveness by being forgiven. They learn about what is right and wrong by what their parents say and do. They learn about how to deal with anger, stress, sadness, and other emotions by the way their parents deal with emotions. They learn about how men and women interact by watching the interaction of their parents.

When parents are negative role models, children absorb their parents' attitudes and behaviors on issues such as drug or alcohol use, smoking, sex, and religion. If they

*are lucky, children from dysfunctional homes find positive
role models outside of their own families that will expose
them to more wholesome values and behaviors.*

*It is possible for children to break the cycle of dys-
function that was passed on to them by their parents.
And while the road is often a difficult one, it can be
smoother if they can make a connection with God and
people of faith who will help them on their journey.*

When Barbara was 11 or 12, they moved to a small
house in Virginia. Her uncle, who had left the Catholic
Church after his divorce, took them to an Episcopal church.
Barbara liked it and started walking to a nearby Episcopal
church on Sunday mornings. The church was a haven from
her home. "We often did not have anything in the refrigera-
tor but my mother's beer," she says. "Her alcoholism caused
her to isolate herself. She would lock herself in her bedroom.
She dragged home low-life men. I wanted out desperately."

Barbara sensed that education would be her ticket to
freedom. She begged her mother to get her into the Catholic
high school. "I never remember my mom going to church,"
she recalls, "but she did go talk to the priest. Somehow I got
a scholarship so that I could go there for the last three years
of high school."

Barbara went through the motions of being a Catholic,
but she did not attend Mass. "In religion class, I learned
the history of the Church, but not much about Jesus or the
Bible," she remembers.

While Barbara was in high school, the court took cus-
tody of one of her brothers after he stole a car. Her other

brother dropped out of school. It made Barbara even more determined to succeed. She worked part-time to pay for her school uniform and clothes. By her senior year, she was a National Merit Scholar and earned a full scholarship to Carnegie Tech. After one semester of college, she dropped out of school to get married.

"I was so emotionally crippled that I could not understand what marriage was," she admits. "I was unfaithful even before we married."

Barbara describes herself as "a countercultural hippie" and "a radical leftist/antiwar activist/radical feminist/abortion-rights fighter." She had three tattoos, dropped acid, and hung out at rock concerts. Her first child was born in 1969, and Barbara named her Samantha Sunshine.

In spite of her wild lifestyle, Barbara wanted to be a good mother. She started to read parenting books and was captivated by *The Absorbent Mind*, by Maria Montessori. Deciding to become a Montessori teacher, Barbara finished college and attended the Montessori Institute. After graduation, she taught for a year in an inner-city school in Washington, DC.

"I see this part of my life as two threads — the negative and the positive," she admits. "I used a lot of drugs, I drank a lot, and I was unfaithful to my husband. But I was trying to be a good mother and to make a difference in the world. It was crazy, I know, but this is what happens when people grow up like I did — with no moral compass."

In 1972, Barbara and her husband moved to San Francisco, and in 1975 they had a second child, Jasmine Moondance. Shortly after Jasmine was born, Barbara became addicted to cocaine. "Cocaine has the effect of making you feel like you can do anything you want," she explains. "I left my husband and Samantha. I took Jasmine with me and became a drug dealer and a welfare mother. I was a destructive force in the lives of everyone with whom I came in contact."

After a year, Barbara's husband threatened to put Samantha into a foster home, so Barbara took her daughter back, but she admits that she was a neglectful mother: "I became what I had sworn never to become. I became my mother: promiscuous, alcoholic, and self-absorbed, bringing strange men in and out of our lives. I even had an abortion during this time." Barbara and her husband eventually divorced.

Barbara's drinking reached a point where she began having blackouts (which means that while she was not unconscious, she would remember nothing about what she said or did). It was unsettling. One morning, she woke up after another blackout, fell to her knees, and cried: "God, please help me. I am an alcoholic!"

Barbara attended her first Alcoholics Anonymous meeting on March 17, 1980, and achieved sobriety through the Twelve Steps of AA. She learned to stay sober one day at a time, to take responsibility for the harm she had done in her past, to make amends, to pay her bills, and to keep her house clean. Drugs and alcohol had allowed Barbara to bury the pain of her past, but now she had to face those demons. She went into therapy and made rapid progress.

Breaking the Cycle of Addiction

Many recovery programs use the Twelve Steps of Alcoholics Anonymous as a framework for their support groups.

> *In the first step, people have to admit that they are powerless over the addiction. Then they turn their lives over to God and gradually begin to focus on their own spiritual growth and development.*
>
> *In subsequent steps, they take a moral inventory of themselves, recognize how their behavior has hurt others, and then take specific steps to atone for what they have done.*
>
> *In the final steps, they strive to strengthen their relationship with God, find ways to reach out to others, and continue to practice the Twelve Steps in every aspect of their lives.*
>
> *If you or someone you know suffers from an addiction, it is important to get help. Priests and pastoral associates themselves may not have the training necessary to help you, but they will know where to refer you. If you want anonymity, you can call your local Catholic Charities office for a referral to a support group in your area.*

In September 1982, Barbara met Tripp Curtis through Alcoholics Anonymous. They shared an interest in New Age spirituality. They read New Age books, listened to tapes, and meditated in an attempt to envision past lives and unlock the secrets of reality. Tripp was six years younger than Barbara and had never been married.

Tripp moved into Barbara's home, and three months later Barbara discovered that she was pregnant. "This was something I regard as a miracle, as I had had a terrible infection during my druggie days, and the doctors told me I would be sterile for the rest of my life," she explains. "I was even using birth control as an added precaution."

When Barbara told Tripp about the pregnancy, he insisted that they get married. The wedding was a New Age ceremony, during which they recited vows at sunset on a deck overlooking the Pacific Ocean. The next few months were rocky. "We were so emotionally crippled and immature!" Barbara admits. "We separated once and were brought back together after seeing the movie *Brother Sun, Sister Moon*, about St. Francis and St. Claire."

Their son, Joshua Gabriel, was born on August 20, 1983. Nine months later, Barbara, who was still using birth control, discovered that she was pregnant again. "Tripp was upset this time," she recalls. "It was so much responsibility for a formerly footloose man still not 30! But I almost lost the baby, and that threatened loss made us both realize how precious life is."

After Matthew Raphael was born, Barbara stopped using birth control. She and Tripp decided that they would be open to as many children as they were intended to have. Eighteen months later, Benjamin Michael was born.

When Barbara and Tripp first married, they did not have much money. But over the years, Tripp, who was an arborist, started a successful business called "Mr. Trees," which employed 25 people. Barbara was a stay-at-home mom who helped to promote the business. "We thought of ourselves as spiritual people," she says. "We were meditating daily and studying things our gurus had written. Tripp had also come from a broken home, but together we had found healing by purposefully creating a Norman Rockwell childhood for our children. We even started going to an Episcopal church on Sundays as one of our spiritual disciplines to help bond our family together."

The only problem was that Barbara and Tripp argued a lot. "Both of us were so intent on creating our own reality that we had never heard of surrender or sacrifice," she explains. "Those things weren't part of the New Age spirituality."

What Is New Age Spirituality?

The New Age movement is not really a religion. It has been defined as a fluid collection of beliefs and practices that incorporates elements of Eastern religions, neopaganism, secular humanism, astrology, Wicca, parapsychology, holistic health, and other postmodern ideas. New Agers are free to adopt whatever elements of the movement they find appealing. There is no New Age clergy, no formal membership requirements, no central organization, and no sacred text that stands apart from the thousands of books and tapes on the subject. Meditation, transcendentalism, and reincarnation tend to be common elements. The movement emerged in the 1970s and takes its name from the Age of Aquarius, which is supposed to bring about a new world order of peace, harmony among people, and an end to war, discrimination, hunger, poverty, pollution, and disease.

One morning, Barbara heard an advertisement for a weekend marriage conference that promised to heal troubled marriages. "I signed us up," she recalls. "This would be my last-ditch effort. If it didn't work, I would make Tripp leave and get a divorce."

It turned out to be a Christian conference, and the first speaker talked about how God's plan for marriage differs from the world's expectations. "They said Satan wanted to destroy marriages," Barbara recalls. "The New Age had no explanation for evil. I had always thought Satan was a myth, but suddenly it made sense: How could two people who were so dedicated to raising a healthy family meet so much resistance within ourselves?"

The next morning, the speaker explained that God has a plan for everyone and that all people need to invite Jesus into their lives. "In typical evangelical fashion, the leaders asked us to make a decision," Barbara recalls. "They prayed the Sinner's Prayer, and we could agree silently in our hearts if we wanted to accept Jesus. I thought: *Oh my goodness! Jesus is not just a spiritual teacher! He is the Son of God! Of course I want to receive Him in my heart!*

"I prayed silently with tears streaming down my face. I looked at Tripp, and he was crying too. We knew something profound had happened — something we had never found in our New Age rituals."

When they got home, they threw away their New Age books and tapes. They began to read the Bible and joined an evangelical church. They also developed a deep disdain for Catholicism, believing that it was a church filled with empty ritual that robbed its followers of a true relationship with Jesus. Barbara taught her children to chant, "Dead church! Dead church!" whenever they drove past a Catholic parish. But even though she was teaching her children that the Catholic Church was dead, she would sit in a tiny Catholic mission church whenever she felt depressed. She would feel

God's presence there in a way she never experienced in the evangelical church.

Over the next few years, Barbara and Tripp had four more children: Zachary, Sophia, Jonny (who has Down's syndrome), and Madeleine. In 1995, they adopted a baby with Down's syndrome so that Jonny would have a brother like himself. After that, two couples asked them to adopt their Down's syndrome children, and Barbara and Tripp agreed, increasing their family to 12 children — four of whom have Down's syndrome.

Barbara homeschooled the children for 10 years. In 1993, she started writing articles for other mothers who wanted to know how she could homeschool while dealing with toddlers and babies. She also began to speak to pro-life groups — not just about abortion, but also about not using birth control and trusting God with your family size. She met many Catholics in her travels, and she began to see Catholicism in a more positive light.

In 2002, Barbara and Tripp sold their ranch and their business in California and moved to Virginia, with their 12 children, 2 sons-in-law, and a growing number of grandchildren. "This was like evangelical heaven," Barbara explains. "We found a church filled with people who trusted God and lived very righteous lives. We were happy, and I wasn't looking for any changes."

During this time, people would assume that the Curtis family was Catholic because it was so large. Barbara would assure them that they were not. In September 2007, however, Barbara was speaking to a group in Maine when she blurted out, "I think I'm going to have to become Catholic because they are the only Christians who are not just antiabortion but completely pro-life!" She could hardly believe those words came out of her mouth. Afterward, several people pressed rosaries into her hands and told her they would pray for her.

What Does the Church Teach About Birth Control?

The fullest explanation of Church teaching on birth control and natural family planning can be found in the encyclical Humanae Vitae *("Of Human Life"), which was written by Pope Paul VI in 1968. In 1993, Pope John Paul II reaffirmed this teaching in the encyclical* Veritatis Splendor *("The Splendor of Truth"). In 2005, Pope Benedict XVI expanded on the real meaning of love and the responsibilities of married couples in his encyclical* Deus Caritas Est *("God Is Love")*

Two months later, the same thing happened when Barbara was speaking at a pro-life banquet in Maryland. The next day, she announced on her blog that she was seriously thinking about returning to the Catholic Church.

"A firestorm erupted, which pretty much sealed the deal," Barbara recalls. "Though my readers knew me, some could not reconcile their prejudice against Catholics. Some argued, some left the blog, some told me I was bound for hell."

In the meantime, Barbara felt compelled to go to Mass. She describes it as similar to her "born-again" experience. "Just as then I had understood Jesus as God's Son, at Mass I felt God illuminating the truth about His Holy Church."

She remembers watching the priest fold the linens after Communion and feeling a universal connection — the same words, the same motions, the same Scriptures — across time and space. Barbara especially loved the quieter, contemplative aspects of the Mass.

"There was something about the church that when you walked in, I could feel my ego and my individuality shrinking," she explains. "It was not just about finding the best pastor or the best youth group or the best worship music. It was about accepting what God has given us, a Church uniquely designed to fit us in our humanness, our brokenness, our need. Every moment seemed filled with meaning and God's love. How could anyone take it for granted?"

She remembers looking at people in the pews around her who obviously were taking their Catholic faith for granted. Suddenly, it was as if God spoke to her heart with these words: *Who are you to judge?*

"In evangelicalism, you can choose a church with people who are very devout and exemplary in their conduct," Barbara explains. "Not so in Catholicism. There is true diversity here — all races, ages, socioeconomic backgrounds, and all levels of understanding and appreciation of faith. It occurred to me that this is how God wanted it. After this, I felt infused with love for all the people in the pews — even those who seemed disinterested. It occurred to me that the evangelical church sets people up to be judgmental and to feel superior based on the things that set us apart rather than the things that bring us together."

Barbara's plan was to go to Mass early each Sunday and then accompany her family to the evangelical church, because she did not want to disrupt anything in their lives.

"I was naive," she admits. "I was not bargaining on anti-Catholic prejudice that others directed toward me. But the prejudice did serve a purpose. My husband, Tripp, who had no Catholic background, was so curious to find out the truth that he began reading the early Church Fathers and came to the conclusion that the Catholic Church was the true Church. He entered RCIA and was received into the Church at the Easter Vigil 2008."

Barbara does not regret her evangelical experience. It was the foundation upon which she established a relationship with Jesus Christ, and it allowed her to eventually move into the fullness of truth in the Catholic Church.

"I completely believe that because of my baptism, God was always watching over me," Barbara explains. "Yes, my life was hard, but that was not God's fault. That was because of original sin. My mom somehow could not rise above her circumstances. But through God's mercy and with His help, I was able to rise above mine."

The Mass has sustained her, especially in the aftermath of her return to Catholicism, as she dealt with the loss of many evangelical friends and backlash from her daughter Samantha, who could not understand why Barbara had to obtain an ecclesiastical annulment of her first marriage.

Barbara appreciated the annulment process. She knew that because of her background and childhood traumas, she had been unable to comprehend the real meaning of marriage, and she was grateful for the opportunity to prove that her first marriage was not valid. It also allowed her to convalidate her union with Tripp, after 25 years of raising her 2 daughters and adding 10 more children to their family.

Barbara also loves the rich tradition of prayers written by saints, and she loves the Rosary, which keeps her focused on the life, passion, and resurrection of Jesus. She encourages people who feel pulled toward the Catholic Church to follow the Holy Spirit.

"Once you begin to entertain the idea that there is one true Church, it doesn't make any sense to be anywhere else," she explains, "and your heart will be restless until you bring it home."

She warns, however, that adult converts and "reverts" (those who return to the Catholic faith) sometimes pay a price. "Many lose friends and family," Barbara says. She continues:

> I lost some of my publishers. Since becoming Catholic, we lost our home to foreclosure. Shortly after that, my husband went in for a routine knee replacement and ended up getting a MRSA infection. He almost lost his leg, and instead of being out of work for a month, he was out for nine months. It left us with very little to live on. But through this time, the Catholic Church carried us. Good Catholics from northern Virginia brought us meals, stocked our pantry, filled our gas tanks, sent us gift cards, and prayed for my husband's healing. I never felt more connected to or dependent on God, who met every need through the Body of Christ. In so many ways, I feel like Catholics really live the Scripture that evangelicals memorize. Catholics seem to understand that suffering is not God's judgment, but His love.

Barbara's husband finally found a job as a school-bus driver, and he sees it as a ministry that allows him to touch the lives of children without fathers. Barbara continues to write her blog, sharing with other mothers her faith, her hope, and her love.

For Additional Information

- Barbara Curtis, *Mommy, Teach Me!: Preparing Your Preschool Child for a Lifetime of Learning* (B&H Publishing Group, 2007).
- Barbara Curtis, *Mommy, Teach Me to Read!: A Complete and Easy-to-Use Home Reading Program* (B&H Publishing Group, 2007).
- Barbara Curtis, *Lord, Please Meet Me in the Laundry Room* (Beacon Hill Press, 2004).
- Barbara Curtis, *The Mommy Manual: Planting Roots That Give Your Children Wings* (Revell, 2005).
- Barbara Curtis, *The Mommy Survival Guide: Making the Most of the Mommy Years* (Beacon Hill Press, 2006).
- Barbara Curtis, *Reaching the Left from the Right: Talking About Social Issues with People Who Don't Think Like You* (Beacon Hill Press, 2006).
- Barbara Curtis, *Dirty Dancing at the Prom and Other Issues Christian Teens Face: How Parents Can Help* (Beacon Hill Press, 2005).

Websites

- Barbara Curtis: *www.barbaracurtis.com*
- Barbara Curtis' blog "Mommy Life": *www.mommylife.net*

Tom Peterson

*Tom Peterson was a successful advertising executive
when he experienced a dramatic conversion that prompted
him to start Catholic media ministries (and the website
CatholicsComeHome.org) that produce and air
powerful television commercials aimed at changing hearts
and minds with the message of life and truth. Tom believes
his vocation is to evangelize using the power of media. He
lives with his wife, Tricia, and their three daughters
in the Atlanta suburbs, where they are
active in their local parish.*

TOM PETERSON grew up in a faith-filled Catholic family. They went to Mass every Sunday, and looking back, he sees nothing missing in his Catholic upbringing. "I loved my faith because my parents loved their faith, and it translated to me," he recalls. "I was trying to be a good kid who did the right things."

By the time he reached junior high school, however, his "good Catholic boy" image ricocheted against him, and other boys began to pick on him, ridicule him, and beat him up. "I think that started my spiral down," Tom admits. "I had it in my heart that I was going to get even with them by becoming successful. I remember saying to myself: *I'm not going to hire you someday.* I look back now and think how foolish it was for me to think that as a teenager. But I carried that into young adulthood, where I was determined to prove something — not only to myself, but to those guys."

Tom Peterson made good on his promise. After graduating from Arizona State College, he landed a high-paying job. He thought about buying a Ferrari but opted for a condo instead. He eventually did buy the sports car, and he would drive 90 mph on Phoenix freeways, swearing at people who got in his way. He eventually started his own advertising agency, and he became even more successful. But along with his success came a distorted sense of pride.

"I was out of control," he explains. "I suffered from 'affluenza.' I was making a couple hundred thousand dollars a year, and I was amassing more and more material stuff in order to fill the emptiness in my heart, but nothing was making me happy. I was addicted to money, power, glory, and the satisfaction that was proving something to myself and to other people."

He married his wife, Tricia, in 1986, and two years later their daughter Katie was born. Two more daughters, Kim and Chris, followed in 1990 and 1995.

There was never any question that Tom and Tricia would raise their daughters in the Catholic faith. He went to Mass every Sunday with his family, but he would daydream through Mass, thinking about what he would eat for lunch or the things he had to do on Monday. "I was there physically, but I was mentally and spiritually absent," he acknowledges.

This feeling of spiritual emptiness bothered Tom. "I think we all know the truth down deep," he explains. "As we get deeper into the deceptions, the lies, the lures of the world that are sold to us, it becomes habitual, and it gets deeper, and suddenly it doesn't feel wrong. It doesn't feel like we have abandoned God. I justified my mediocrity and my lack of faith by saying, 'I'm not as bad as other people are!' But in reality, I was immersed in materialism, consumerism, and secularism."

Tom was actually listening at Mass one Sunday when a young man invited the men of the parish to attend a Cursillo retreat. "I actually wanted to go," he recalls, "and I couldn't think of any excuse for not going."

What Is a Cursillo Retreat?

A Cursillo retreat is an intensely spiritual weekend of renewal that brings participants to a deeper commitment to their faith and a new understanding of what it means to live as a disciple of Jesus Christ. The movement began in Spain in the late 1940s and was introduced in the United States in the 1960s. The word cursillo *means "little course." Cursillo retreats are offered in many dioceses throughout the United States. For additional information, contact the National Cursillo Center at* www.cursillo.org.

On the first evening of the retreat, the priest invited men with "prayer language" to come into another room for a short meeting. Tom wasn't sure what that meant, but he decided to find out what they were doing. When he walked into the room, there was one empty chair. *There's a chair for you if you want it*, he remembers thinking.

During the brief meeting, the priest suggested that they would pray over the other men during Benediction. He reminded them that the Holy Spirit would work through them. "God will be God, and we will be His instruments," the priest said.

Later that evening, the priest asked if anyone wanted to be prayed over, and Tom was the first one to jump up. "I really felt as if I needed something," he recalls. "They prayed over me, and I dropped down on the floor in front of the Eucharist. I literally heard God say to me: *Downsize and simplify*. I knew instantly what He meant. I had so many homes and cars. I had so many things. But I didn't have time for God. Then the Lord started ministering to me: *You've got one foot in My world and one foot in the secular world. You're trying to have it both ways. You need to choose sides. Do you want to follow Me? Do you want to be on My side?* I said: *Absolutely. One hundred percent!* And in that instant, my life changed."

The first thing Tom promised God was that he would not be a cheap Catholic anymore. "I was making a lot of money, and I was only putting two dollars in the collection each week. I said: *Lord, it's all Your money. I realize now that You've blessed me with it. I'm going to write a check when I get back from the retreat.*"

A few days after the retreat, Tom learned that his biggest client was a white-collar criminal. He thought: *I can't be a part of this. I know the truth now.* He resigned from the account and asked that they donate the $70,000 they owed him to charity.

Several weeks later, Tom caught his partner cheating business clients out of money. "I can't be part of this," he told his partner, and he walked away from a business that was netting $500,000 a year. He never felt freer in his life. He remembers praying: *Jesus, I trust in You. Whatever You want, I will do.*

The first thing on Tom's agenda was his promise to downsize and simplify. He sold his vacation home, several cars, and other unnecessary possessions. His wife, Tricia, who had gone on a women's retreat the following weekend, stood behind him all the way.

"She didn't care about all the stuff," Tom explains. "She cared about doing the right thing. God gave us what we need-ed to get out of that addiction of materialism. When we gave it up, we realized we had entered into a greater adventure."

Tom started reading the Bible, and phrases would stick in his head. He began to feel a deep desire to go to daily Mass. Each morning, he would ask himself: *Should I go to Mass or to work?* The words "Seek first the kingdom of God and all these things will be added to you" (see Matthew 6:33) would echo in his mind. He discovered that when he went to Mass, his whole day went well.

Tom also heard the words "To whom much is given, much is expected" (see Luke 12:48). He became an ex-traordinary minister of the Eucharist, and he volunteered to sponsor someone in the RCIA (Rite of Christian Initiation of Adults). It was through the RCIA that he became im-mersed in the Catholic faith, and his relationship with Jesus grew stronger.

"I was on the path of learning," Tom recalls, "and I knew God had a plan for me, but what was it?"

Learning More About Your Faith

Many, if not most, people coming back to the Church feel a deep desire to learn more about their Catholic faith. For many people, formal religious education stopped at around an eighth-grade level. If you feel that you have some catching up to do, call your diocesan office to find out what kinds of adult-education opportunities are available on a diocesan level and in parishes. You may be surprised at the variety of adult-education opportunities that are open to you.

You might want to join a Scripture study or a faith-sharing group. You might want to take a course at a local seminary or Catholic college. There are also opportunities to learn more about your Catholic faith on the Internet.

Once you start down the path of learning, you may be surprised at where the journey takes you!

Tom felt as if he had found a treasure chest full of spiritual gold, and he wanted to tell everybody. "I had a sales and marketing background," he explains. "I was a guy who promoted stuff or services that made me money. But now I had found the best thing in the universe — God, Jesus, and the Holy Spirit — and I wanted to tell everybody what the Blessed Trinity had done in my life."

One morning at Mass, Tom asked God to please let him bring someone closer to Christ. After Mass, a woman tapped him on the shoulder and asked if he could help her son who had been away from the Church for 20 years. So Tom visited the young man several times and invited him to come to Mass, but the young man refused. Several months later, the young man called Tom and said he had changed his mind because he had been fishing that day and pulled a crucifix out of the water. He wondered if it was a sign. The young man started coming to church, and a few months later he met the girl of his dreams.

A short time later, Tom had two dreams of his own that would lead him in a new direction. The first was about a little baby being suffocated, and Tom knew that he was being called to help her. In the second dream, he was producing some sort of Catholic film. He responded to what he believed God was asking by making several pro-life commercials and setting up a website for women who were considering abortion. "I knew nothing about it, but God was going to teach me," he recalls.

The commercials began to air, and young women started contacting the website Tom had established at PregnancyLine.org for help. Over the years, Tom made new commercials, which now air nationally on MTV, Black Entertainment Television, and E! Tom estimates that thousands of babies have been saved through God's grace.

God was using the gifts and talents Tom had developed in his secular career to reach out to pregnant women, but there was another gift that Tom was destined to share. He knew what it felt like to be spiritually numb, and he had experienced the joy of reconnecting with the Catholic faith. Tom would use this experience of conversion to reach out to others who had drifted away from their faith.

As part of the Jubilee Year in 2000, Tom worked with the Diocese of Phoenix to create commercials and a website called "CatholicsComeHome.org" that invited people to come back to the Church. The commercials capture the history, beauty, spirituality, and universality of the Catholic faith. The website addresses the issues that are of concern to people who are away from the Church. Within a few weeks of the commercials airing on local television, thousands of people responded. Mass attendance increased, and priests reported that people who had been away from the Church for years were coming to confession.

What's Great About the Catholic Church

In the commercial entitled "Epic," Tom Peterson captured the essence of the Catholic Church on both a universal and a personal level. Using powerful images, the commercial explains that the Catholic Church was founded by Jesus Christ and that it has spanned the world for centuries, with an unbroken chain of leaders that has continued for over 2,000 years. The Catholic Church has established schools, hospitals, orphanages, and charitable organizations that help the poor. It founded the college system, developed the scientific method and laws of evidence, and compiled the Bible. "Epic" shows the viewer how every hour of every day a Mass is celebrated somewhere in the world, with Catholics sharing in the Eucharist. The commercial invites people who feel separated from the Church to come home.

"Epic" is a powerful reminder of all that is good and holy in our Catholic faith tradition. To view the commercial, log onto www.catholicscomehome.org.

Catholics Come Home is now partnering with dioceses all over the country to invite people back to the Church.

"I am absolutely thrilled that God chose me to be on this adventure," Tom says. "It is giving us a chance to penetrate the secular media and let people know that we have Jesus Himself in the Eucharist and that the Church is His bride. When these ads air on television, they stand out like light in the darkness. People get excited about being Catholic. The ads restore enthusiasm for the Catholic faith in the way the secular world can understand. We present the truth in a loving way."

Today, when people ask Tom what he does, he pulls out his Blackberry and shows them the commercials. It's not unusual for people to admit they are former Catholics. Tom follows up by giving them the website address. Most of the time, he never finds out if the person comes back to the Church, but he doesn't care. He believes that God is simply asking him to plant the seed and that the Holy Spirit can make it grow.

"There's the famous painting where Jesus is knocking on the door, and there's no doorknob, which means we have to open it from the inside," Tom says. "That was me. I invited Jesus in, and He changed my life forever. I'm hooked. Nothing brings me greater joy than knowing that I am here to love and serve God."

Websites

- Virtue Media: *www.virtuemedia.org*
- Catholics Come Home: *www.catholicscomehome.org*
- Encourage Priests: *www.encouragepriests.org*
- Pregnancy Line: *www.pregnancyline.org*

AFTERWORD
An Invitation to Consider Coming Home

IF YOU EXPERIENCED A DEEP SPIRITUAL LONGING as you read the stories in this book, you can be sure that it is the pull of the Holy Spirit. Whether or not you recover your Catholic faith is your choice.

Like all of the people in this book, if you decide to return, you will experience twists and turns along the way. The route you take will be as unique and as personal as your own story:

- Maybe you will start to go to daily Mass for a while before you decide to come back completely.
- Or you might decide to not go to Mass at first but instead attend a parish lecture series or join a parish Scripture study.
- You might begin by spending time in a Eucharistic Adoration chapel.
- Or you might get involved in the parish food pantry or outreach center.
- You might begin to read your way back into the Church, as many people in this book did.
- Or you might wrestle your way back through conversations with a priest, a deacon, or someone else who is willing to help you sort through some of the things that are bothering you.
- You could sign up for a parish ministry such as Catholics Returning Home or Landings.

- Maybe you will spontaneously decide to stop at a Catholic church on a Saturday afternoon and go to confession.
- Or you might choose to make an appointment to meet with a priest.
- If you have marriage issues to deal with, you might need to look into the possibility of applying for a Church annulment.
- You might find that you will have to engage in some serious talks about faith if your spouse does not share your interest in becoming part of the Catholic Church.
- You might have to explain to family members and friends why you have decided to return to the faith of your baptism. And you might discover that some of your relationships will be strained.

No matter what happens along your journey, it will be an adventure the likes of which you've never experienced before. It will be an adventure into the depths of your soul, where you will experience God in a new and different way. You will have the opportunity to develop a personal relationship with Jesus Christ. You will have the opportunity to make an adult faith commitment.

If you decide that you want to return to the Catholic Church, it is really important to become a member of a parish. You might want to shop around for a parish — even if you have to drive a little bit — before you decide to formally register. Different parishes have different personalities. Look for a parish where you feel connected.

The Order of the Mass will be the same everywhere, but the music and other nonessentials may differ. Some parishes will have traditional liturgies. Some will seem more contemporary. Some will be community oriented and welcoming. Others will be quiet and reverent.

You will also meet different kinds of Catholics in different parishes. They will have different intellectual levels, different socioeconomic backgrounds, and different ways of living as Catholic Christians. You will find conservatives and liberals, good Catholics and "not-so-good" Catholics, active Catholics and passive Catholics. Some will have special devotions to Our Lady or a particular saint. Others will focus on social-justice issues or outreach to the poor.

No matter what kind of parish you choose, remember that the Catholic Church puts you in touch with wisdom and truth that is thousands of years old. You will discover the presence of Christ in the celebration of the Mass, in receiving the Eucharist, in Scripture, in personal prayer, and in your relationship with other Catholics. You will find that your faith will support you in times of joy and in times of sorrow. Other people will touch your life in the Catholic Church, and you will touch theirs. You will experience the peace of Christ that the world cannot give. You will find that there is meaning and purpose in your life.

All of this, and much more, is waiting for you in the Catholic Church. Maybe it's time for you to recover your Catholic faith.

INDEX OF SIDEBARS

About the Author

LORENE HANLEY DUQUIN has been active in ministry to inactive and alienated Catholics since 1992 in the Diocese of Buffalo. She has conducted lectures and workshops in parishes and at national and diocesan conferences in the United States and Canada.

Lorene's articles have appeared in a variety of secular and Catholic publications. She is the author of several pamphlets on evangelization topics for Our Sunday Visitor including *Top Ten Reasons to Come Back to the Church* and *When Someone Is Hurt by the Church*. Some of her books include *Seeking an Annulment with the Help of Your Catholic Faith, A Century of Catholic Converts, When a Loved One Leaves the Church,* and *Could You Ever Come Back to the Catholic Church?*

Lorene has four adult children and three grandchildren.